Viv was born in   f four children. She is married to Martyn a... n they have five children and twelve grandchildren. After a varied career from Shop Assistant, to Business Analyst to Lecturer, Viv decided to follow her first love, writing.

To: Jan

Thank you

Viv xxx

This book is dedicated to my dad, Harry Booth. It was supposed to be a different dedication to you in a different book but hey ho, that is life. You did so like to tell 'tall tales', I just carried the tradition on and wrote it down instead. Thanks for the 'story' gene, Dad.

This book is also dedicated to my three girls, Natalie, Lauren and Yasmin; you have always been and always will be my greatest achievement.

Viv Booth

I Do Not Want a Fish Finger Sandwich

Austin Macauley Publishers

LONDON • CAMBRIDGE • NEW YORK • SHARJAH

Copyright © Viv Booth 2023

The right of Viv Booth to be identified as author of this work has been asserted by the author in accordance with sections 77 and 78 of the Copyright, Designs and Patents Act 1988.

All rights reserved. No part of this publication may be reproduced, stored in a retrieval system, or transmitted in any form or by any means, electronic, mechanical, photocopying, recording, or otherwise, without the prior permission of the publishers.

Any person who commits any unauthorised act in relation to this publication may be liable to criminal prosecution and civil claims for damages.

This is a work of fiction. Names, characters, businesses, places, events, locales, and incidents are either the products of the author's imagination or used in a fictitious manner. Any resemblance to actual persons, living or dead, or actual events is purely coincidental.

A CIP catalogue record for this title is available from the British Library.

ISBN 9781398497160 (Paperback)
ISBN 9781035800322 (ePub e-book)

www.austinmacauley.com

First Published 2023
Austin Macauley Publishers Ltd®
1 Canada Square
Canary Wharf
London
E14 5AA

Thank you to all my family and friends, old and new for their continued support and who define this book. Without you, there would be no story.

Table of contents

Pain in the Bum or Just a Bit Odd	12
Educating Peter	28
Blame Is a Clever Trickster	60
Sheffield Hallam University 1993	85
Phare and Away	93
I Did Not Learn This at School	128
Norfolk N Good	158
Slow You Down	176

It is not a bad life; it is just a bad day.

Pain in the Bum or Just a Bit Odd

Oldham 1960s

Have you ever, ever, ever, in your long-legged life
Seen a long-legged fella with a long-legged wife
No, I've never, ever, ever in my long-legged life
Seen a long-legged fella with a long-legged wife
No, I have not either.

I suppose I like this rhyme because there is no way I am ever, ever, ever going to have long legs, never mind legs that are even the same size, I just pretend that I have. I do not like to admit it but having odd-sized legs does sometimes cause me problems. Not so much when we are playing double-Dutch skipping, but it is a big problem when we play the French version. This game is where you tie together a load of elastic bands and connect into a big loop and then two people get inside the circle with the bands placed firstly around their ankles. The contestant then performs a series of manoeuvres before moving onto the next level, the calves. I have got no chance, apart from the odd legs, I am a bit small; by the time the loop is at their thighs, it might as well be around my neck. Balance and co-ordination is definitely not my strong point.

It is the same really with any physical activity I try, I have no technique but an awful lot of enthusiasm, too much sometimes. My aunty who is the wardrobe mistress on Eastbourne Pier comes to visit us and she always brings me stuff that the dancers have left behind, like old ballet and tap shoes. I was allowed the ballet shoes until that fateful day I attempted an intricate pirouette at the top of the stairs and landed in a heap at the bottom. It is a miracle I have managed to keep hold of the tap shoes because I am driving everyone mad tip tapping on the flags in the backyard. I seem to annoy people quite regularly.

I love dancing and so want to be in the majorettes and shake my pompoms in the Oldham Carnival, but no, I have one leg shorter than the other and I might fall over. Originally, Oldham Carnival was part of Oldham Wakes, the major event celebrated throughout the whole town, with different dates within August for Oldham, Shaw, Failsworth etc. Rush carts were decorated with borrowed ornaments and paraded through the town accompanied by brightly dressed dancers and crowds of supporters. This became the forerunner for my carnival which I am allowed to watch; we normally stand near the 82/98 bus stop facing Oldham Parish Church but I have never danced in it.

It is always the same reply, "You cannot have a bicycle you have one leg shorter than the other and you might fall off." I am allowed to go to Brownies, but it is not really the same thing.

My playground is Drury Lane where we live, up Under Street, Under Lane, Colin Croft and Asia Fields. The spare land on Upper Lane is my favourite venue. Each year, the fairground comes to this piece of land and it usually lasts for a few days. It is placed next to the stumps where we play shops, usually a bakery like Vickers' and we use the stones as the shop counter and mud pies for buns. This is where I made my greatest find. There is a machine at the fair which has a sort of a desert scene with camels moving through it with a tray attached to their backs. If you put a six-pence in the machine, a box would fall onto one of the trays and then the camel will move around the scene and deposit the box down a hole. You then get your prize, possibly a ring, not like those moulded plastic ones you get in crackers or I got when I got engaged to Richard Flint when I was eight, but a much better model, gold and everything. Well, the fair has gone but they have left a load of boxes out of the machine and some still have prizes in them! Well, I only get a three-penny bit for my spends, so this is like finding a treasure trove.

When the fair goes to the next venue, it also leaves behind a couple of travellers in their caravans at the top of the land near Manchester Road. We are a bit wary of them and we normally keep as far away as possible from their location but for some mad reason we—Lynne, Anne and me—have decided to play knock-a-door runaway with them; I think our find must have addled our brains or something. There were two caravans remaining, both very ornate and grand, so we crept up along the side of one of them making sure we bob down under the windows so they could not see us. At the door of the caravan, we all three of us knocked on the door in unison and then turned to run away. As quick as a flash, a woman was out of the door and was running down the spare land chasing us with a dirty great big carving knife in her hand. She was shouting something, swearing I think, but I was not staying around to find out what.

My brother is not smiling at me at the moment, it is more like a grimace, he might even be swearing. He has manfully agreed to bring me to Heron Street baths for the first time. I have always thought the baths were miles away but it has not taken too long to get here. As you walk into the building, the swimming pool is directly in front of you and at either side of the entrance is a normal brown tiled bath. Parallel to these are two rows of cubicles with green curtains, a row for the boys and one for the girls. When I asked my dad about the brown baths, he told me that they were for people who did not have that kind bathing facility at home; I found that very strange. Public baths had become popular in Oldham by the mid-nineteenth century and the first public baths were opened on Union Street in 1854 at a cost of four thousand pounds. It was very successful and by 1861 over thirty-five thousand people used the baths. This presented a problem as the baths became overcrowded, the council struggled to keep the water clean enough to swim in as a thick scum formed overnight. It was decided to build more swimming baths and ban the use of soap in the main bath and so Heron Street Baths were built in 1889 with the separate brown baths for washing with soap.

"Find a cubicle and get undressed."

I have walked up and down the girl's cubicles and they were all either full of people or their clothes they had left behind on the wooden seats while they went to swim.

What should I do?

I do not think my mum would like me to get changed with girls I do not know. I have stood here at the side of the pool contemplating this problem whilst watching everyone having fun and I have decided to get changed in the girl's toilet. This I have done and I am now standing here in my swimsuit whilst holding my possessions firmly in my hands. The attendant is shouting something at me, I think he is swearing and he does look a bit angry, but I cannot hear him for all the screaming and shouting. I have flicked my head around, put my nose up in the air and ignored him. Hooray! My swimming partner has just come out of his cubicle ready for a swim and is for some reason stood rooted to the spot staring at me from the other side of the swimming pool with a very strange expression on his face. I have smiled and waved but he is still glaring at me, *'What have I done now?'* He looks mortified and he will not look any of his friends in the eye. He has just rushed across, took my clothes off me and put them in the nearest cubicle and dragged me roughly into the pool. *'What is wrong with him? Turns out, he thinks I have undressed at the side of the pool in full view of everyone including his friends. Fool.'*

Oldham Early 1970s

In November 1969, Mum had her first heart attack.

"Vivienne, can you put me some of your blue eye shadow on?" Mum asked.

I am twelve and I have started taking an interest in make-up, not that it makes me look any older; I still look about five. I have one of those bright blue push up crème eye shadow lipstick things. We are both stood in front of the living room fire; Mum and Dad are going out to the Cott Club and for some reason, I am in a 'mood'. Mum just has eye shadow on her lid bit at the bottom of her eye; she never wears mascara, just eyeshadow and a bit of lipstick. It is quite tricky putting it on her actually as her skin is a bit loose and it keeps sticking on the end of the lipstick thing.

"You don't want me to go, do you?" She said in more of a statement than a question.

I have not answered her; I have stomped into the kitchen. I feel a bit silly now, I really wanted a kiss before they went. She is not here; I have run down the lobby and into the street but she has gone.

I will never see her again; she died tonight aged fifty-three.

Dad is helping out at the Philo Pub again tonight. I do not mind really as I get to go and have a glass of lemonade and see Sheba. Sheba is an Alsatian puppy the owners of the pub have bought as a guard dog; she is all white and she is beautiful. I am allowed to take her for a walk every night after school and it feels like she is actually mine. I have always wanted a dog and this is probably the nearest I will get to having one.

I am in the men's urinals in the pub backyard. The owner's grandchildren have already taken Sheba for a walk tonight but they let her off her lead too soon and she has run onto Manchester Road and under a bus. She is here in the toilets wrapped in an old piece of tarpaulin with one of her beautiful white paws sticking out. I just keep standing here, staring at that paw.

Dad has let me have a dog of my own. He is an Alsatian, a normal coloured one and I have called him Red; he is supposed to be a pedigree. Pedigree my foot, I am more pedigree than he is.

I have never looked after a dog before and we always some scrape or other. I love animals; I have household pets, but I also seem to acquire others. y bridge on Drury Lane and if any pigeons or other type of birds fall out of their nests, I will take them home. It has got to the point that if my dad is walking under the bridge and finds one out of the nest, he will bring it home, it saves time because I will bring it back anyway. At one point, I had two pigeons living in a cage in the bathroom. I think I have gone a bit too far this time, I have just spent ages digging a family of feral kittens out of the railway embankment on the way to Asia Fields. They were very determined not to come with me and I was just as determined they would; I am covered in scratches but I have got them all. I have just marched triumphantly home with them wriggling in my arms. My dad is not impressed, he has shaken his head and pointed to the door and said, "Take them back!"

I think he is smiling, but I am not sure.

My dad is in hospital; I am not allowed to visit, of course, he is on the free-list thing and I have had a bit of a strop. I am watching telly waiting for the others to come back; I can hear voices I think they must be here.

Someone has just said that Dad has died in the hospital. I have screamed twice. I have never screamed before in my life; it just seems to be the right thing to do.

I am going to live in Sheffield with my sister; I cannot take Red.

Sheffield 1972

"Don't sit her there, bring her here with us."

I am stood in a classroom; well, I think it is a classroom, it is not like any I have been in before. Instead of the neat rows of desks and chairs that were the rule at Chadderton Grammar School for Girls, these desks are strewn around the room.

at these desks are, in what is supposed to be uniform are higgledy-piggledy groups of girls and BOYS. It feels as though every single one is staring at me, which is probably true.

This is my first day at senior school in Sheffield; I am fifteen.

I have no idea what Sheffield is like other than it is really big. I have been to Sheffield before to stay with my sister but also to visit friends of my dad whom he met in the war; they lived in Attercliffe. This visit stayed in my mind for a long time for two reasons. Firstly, we could not get in the front door, we knocked and we heard movement but nothing happened. After a period of knocking, my dad's friend appeared from round the bottom of the ginnel, or jenal, I think they call it round here, and beckoned us in. We went in by the back door; well, I could not understand it until we went into their front room and a dirty great big sideboard was placed across the back of the front door.

"Dad, what if there's a fire?" I asked bemused.

"Shut up," came the response, Dad pronouncing every word precisely; I knew I was in trouble now.

The second reason I remember the visit is linked to this amazing knack I have of getting into trouble without any intention and it really put me in the dog house, as usual. I was a bit bored because they just kept talking about the war, so they kindly said I could play with some of the toys they had there for their grandchildren. I decided I would take them up on their offer.

I picked up a skipping rope and headed for the backdoor with my dad's whispered words 'behave yourself' ringing in my ears. I think it must have been their backyard that distracted me and got me into trouble; it was nothing like ours in Oldham. We have separate backyards for each house in the terrace with a long back running the full length of all the houses. Here, it seemed to be one backyard shared by four houses, and to be honest, I did not know which bit I was allowed to skip on and which I was not; I was also mindful of my father's words. Anyway, that is my excuse for what happened to the skipping rope. It was (being the operative word) a multi-coloured plastic one with bells in the middle of the synthetic end and I was trying a triple salchow or something similar because I dropped the end of the rope. At first, thank goodness, it appeared to be ok, but then I heard the sickening sound of splintering plastic, oh no, I am in for it now. Dad was not pleased with me and said that I always had to do something that meant he could never take me back. Well, that was a bit rich, it was only a skipping rope and anyway I was not that bothered about going back there; they were all back to front and we would probably be burnt to death in any case.

So, here I am, back in Sheffield stood with Mr Giles, my new teacher, who seems very nice, friendly and approachable, in front of my new classmates at Abbeydale Grange School. This must be what being at a comprehensive school is like. He is nothing like the teachers at my old school and the headmaster when meeting me seemed amazed that I am wearing a full school uniform; looking at this classroom, I think I know why.

Mr Giles laughed at the comments and took me to sit with them. I just do not know what to say and just keep looking at them. They probably think I am a bit peculiar. Just as I thought I was getting to grips with what they were actually saying to me and the 'Chuffin idiot' and the 'Gi'ors' are starting to be strangely familiar, they have all stood up. We are going to assembly and they have formed a single line; this feels familiar, I will just play it by ear and follow them.

Wrong.

I have followed them into the hall and rather than us being in a horizontal line like I am used to, we are lined up the hall vertically and as I joined the line last because I did not have a clue what was happening, I am at the front of the hall. Now, I understand why they all rushed out of the classroom.

They have now started singing hymns and I think I must have landed on an alien planet. I do not know a single tune. I have tried to join in and look as though I know what I am doing but I am not doing a very good job as it is very difficult to mime to something you do not know. I do not think it matters; I am not being watched like a hawk to see if I am singing, or sitting ladylike or facing forward as I should. The teachers do not seem to be bothered about me; they all seem to have their own favourite person to watch.

Now, to the lessons, oh my word. In Maths, we are not even doing the same sums, they are focusing on Algebra where as I was doing Statistics until last week. It is even worse in History; I have been doing Napoleon and they are doing The First World War. I have to sit out in the corridor on my own and just try to understand what I am supposed to be doing without any help at all. English and Art are even more of a nightmare as the marks are based on the work you have done through the last eighteen months; my work is back in Oldham. So, it now appears I am expected to do all that work again in six months, fat chance. And I have to say I think this Art teacher is not normal, he keeps asking me questions that are leaving me gobsmacked.

We are discussing the issue around the work for my portfolio and he has asked, "So, how good are you then?"

"Pardon," I gulped.

"I said how good are you? You must be reasonable because you are taking Art as a chosen subject."

"I, I, I don't know," I stuttered in response.

"Oh, come on, you must do," he persisted, "are you very good, good, not bad, what?"

I am staring at him incredulously and with no little embarrassment. I have never been asked my opinion by a teacher before in my life. Well, in fact, I had never been asked my opinion by any one at all. Surely, he does not want me to be so unladylike as to blow my own trumpet.

"Ok," I mumbled whilst staring at him as if his head is on backwards.

I really think things cannot get any worse.

Wrong.

Along has come the games lesson, at least it is only girls and no boys. Now, I have never been sporty but I have been even less expedient in sports that I have never played before in my life. Tennis! Oh god! To add to my total humiliation, it is with two girls who play cricket for England and who can master any sport on earth. I have just spent the whole lesson running around the court like an idiot and I have never hit any of the balls even when it was my turn to serve.

Thank goodness, that is over, we are now off to get changed and to my surprise and relief, they do not have showers. I do not have the indignity of running through them trying to hide the fact that I actually have nothing to hide. The changing room is a shed next to the field, well I think it is a porta cabin but it seems more like a shed to me.

I have to say the whole games fiasco has gone from bad to worse. From basketball where I can bounce the ball for a maximum of one bounce before getting my feet in the way and kicking it down the full length of the court. To trampolining where I thought I might have some slight advantage with all that jumping up and down in Blackpool whilst on holiday, but no. I am expected to perform a somersault which is definitely not in my repertoire of bottom and knee bounces.

As if the lessons are not bad enough, we keep changing classrooms and I have no idea of where they are or the layout of the school. I keep going the wrong way and stumbling across snogging couples in dark corners who should also be in class, and more to the point, I am more confused as to why they are being allowed to stay where they are.

Sheffield is really BIG.

School life has carried on at its bewildering best, my Mock O levels have been an un-mitigated disaster. The sports lessons have continued to be a complete nightmare and on a purely personal level I appear to have the sexual attraction of a gnat. All the other girls have boyfriends or at least someone who fancies them; I have neither. There are boys that I like but they appear to have no idea that I even exist, one in particular David is in my Maths class. I spend the whole time when not doing my sums, staring longingly at him with nothing but total indifference to me coming back from him.

I have now started a Saturday job as a checkout assistant at Prestos on Ecclesall Road. I really enjoy meeting new people and I love the fact that I am earning money but I do not know if I am cut out for this post. I do keep having a few problems with the till and the conveyor belt. I have just nearly given some poor woman a heart attack as I have tried to charge her six pounds per tin of peas instead of the six pence I should have typed in.

The conveyor belt is just as bad; I have had several incidents with it but today's incident has been the worse. For some reason as I typed in the price for a bag of frozen peas (these incidents always seem to be linked to peas) and laid it flat to go down the conveyor belt, it has got stuck between the belt and the end of the checkout. I have panicked I cannot deny it. I do not know if there is a way of turning the conveyor off, there must be but I do not know where it is or how to do it. So, I am just stood here going, "Ooh, Oooh, oooooooh" and flapping my arms around like a demented pigeon whilst the bag has got tighter and tighter until it could take no more. I am now running around trying to protect everyone with my body whilst frozen peas are being shot like bullets out of the conveyor belt at innocent passers-by.

Walsh's Department Store 1973

I started a new job today at Walsh's Department Store. I have taken my O Levels which were a carbon copy of my mocks, rubbish; so, working full time is the next logical step.

The original Walsh's Department Store had been blitzed in the war and re-opened in 1953 next to the 'Hole in the Road' on Arundel Gate. It is where the posh people shop apparently; I do not know anything about that or about department stores, the nearest thing I know in Oldham is Woolworths.

I was interviewed by Mrs Gent; I do not have a clue what she asked me but I must have made a good impression as she offered me the job. I was to start on the Monday as the junior on the Lighting Department and I had to report to her at nine o'clock.

It is now nine o' clock on Monday and I am a bit nervous, Mrs Gent has just brought me down to the Lighting Department, in the staff lift, of course, and I have been introduced with the words, "I've got a nice little girl for you."

There is my boss Mrs French (Cynthia) and the Saturday/Monday lady Mrs Scott (Ivy), I am not allowed to call them by their first names which feels strangely familiar and comforting. Mrs French is very posh and professional, but nice, Mrs Scott is nice but I think she is a bit wary of me. I have lost count of the times I have said in my head, "You learn something new every day," because everything today is new. My existing knowledge of light fittings is limited to the lamp I won on the bingo on the pier. By the end of the day, I am exhausted, I have never had to stand up all day before and I have to go back again tomorrow.

Today, my second day, I have been introduced to the other member of the staff on the department, Mrs Nelson (Bea), she is nice too but she seems a bit distant.

I have now worked my first two-week rota, Monday to Saturday and then Monday to Friday, with a late night on the second Wednesday, I have now got three days off. Thank goodness, I am absolutely shattered; I do not know who my legs belong to but it certainly is not me and I am trying to remember such strange things like the difference between a small and large burnet cap.

I am back again today and this afternoon Mrs Nelson has asked me to go with her to the loading bay to take a light fitting packed in a great big box to be collected by a customer. People pull up outside Walsh's to collect their goods because they think it makes them look posh. One lady comes every Wednesday afternoon in her chauffeur-driven limousine to collect her shopping, she has even had a bobbin of cotton delivered to her just so her neighbours can see where she shops.

I do not much like the loading bay, it is always freezing cold and dimly lit, also it is the domain of Derek, he is in charge and he seems to have a soft spot for me. He still lives with his mum who I have seen and looks very posh, and she chooses his clothes for him to wear each day. How I came by this information, I do not know. He is always very colour co-ordinated but his shirt will be stripy, his trousers checked and his tie spotty, he always wears a tie. He is very tall and he is not fat but his body looks like it has had all the bones removed from it and as soon as he sees me, envelopes me in a cuddle and I just seem to be lost somewhere inside the mass. Thank goodness, Derek is not here at the moment and as we are standing waiting, Mrs Nelson has started talking to me.

"I really like that song Hey Sue," she stated, I suppose she is trying to find common ground.

"I don't think I know that one," I replied a bit puzzled.

"Course you do," she replied confidently.

"Well, I don't think so, who is it by? Do you think you could sing a bit?" I asked.

She said it is by the Beatles and to my utter astonishment she has started singing it here and now on the loading bay,

"Hey, Sue, don't make it bad, take a sad song and make it better."

I just stood looking at her and something very unusual has happened, I have started to laugh.

"What?" She asked.

"Nothing," I stuttered.

"No, there is something, what?" She enquired smiling at me.

"It's, Hey Jude, not Hey Sue," I giggled.

Again, to my utter astonishment, she has started laughing too, "Oh well, it doesn't matter, it sounds same."

I just looked at her and she looked at me and we have both gone into whoops of laughter. We are laughing so hard we are crying and holding onto each other giggling like mad.

Oh, my god, she gets me!

I have not got in trouble, annoyed her or offended her, we are actually on the same wavelength. Maybe this working lark is going to be better than what I thought.

Educating Peter

Walsh's Department Store 1974

I have taken to this like a duck to water.

I am not saying it has all been plain sailing. I have shorted some poor woman's whole house with my inadequate chandelier wiring; however, health and safety measures are in now place. I currently get Alfred, the electrician down in the basement to check all my work before releasing any light fittings on the unsuspecting public. I do also keep startling customers, literally, with my unusual capacity to static electric shock anyone who comes within a few inches of me, I think myself and the nylon in the carpet are the perfect couple.

I have also mastered the pneumatic cash system, although sometimes I genuinely hate it. The system is used to whizz money and invoices from the shop floor up into the cash office on the fourth floor (which is labelled 'third floor', very confusing) and then any change and customer receipt back down again. This is achieved by blowing or sucking the cash canister through the tubes. You get an empty metal canister which is in the shape of a tube about nine inches long and about three inches in diameter, with padding on the top and bottom. You then twist it to open a little door on the front of the canister and then place the money and invoice inside, then twist again to close the door. You then lift the latch of the door on the wall to the pneumatic system, it is very noisy. Then, you hope that it is sucking and not blowing because if it is doing the latter, your canister will not go up the tube but more importantly, it means there is one coming down the other way and if you do not remove your hand sharpish, you are hit on the knuckles by a flying metal canister, which really hurts. UNDER NO CIRCUMSTANCES are you allowed to leave your post when canisters are whizzing in either direction.

So, this is causing me a slight problem today because I have some very strange man standing next to me, well very close to me, staring at me and quoting Shakespeare:

> *Shall I compare thee to a summer's day?*
> *Thou art more lovely and more temperate:*
> *Rough winds do shake the darling buds of May,*
> *And summer's lease hath all too short a date:*
> *Sometime too hot the eye of heaven shines,*
> *And often is his gold complexion dimm'd;*
> *And every fair from fair sometimes declines,*
> *By chance, or nature's changing course, untrimm'd*
> *But thy eternal summer shall not fade,*
> *Nor lose possession of that fair thou owest;*
> *Nor shall Death brag thou wander'st in his shade,*
> *When in eternal lines to time thou growest;*
> *So long as men can breathe, or eyes can see,*
> *So long lives this, and this gives life to thee.*

I know it is Shakespeare, well it sounds like it but the problem is I am not allowed to move away from the system as my cash and receipt maybe at this very moment hurtling back down towards me. This man is weird! I would say he is in his thirties and is a businessman, why do I think that? Because he is wearing a grey three-piece suit, shirt and tie. However, that is where the businessman impression ends because over the top of this apparel, he is wearing a ladies' pink rain mac which appears to be four sizes too small for him AND he is quoting poetry or something to me.

I have never been so relieved to get my knuckles rapped and to get out from behind that column in the Hardware Department.

Apart from this and those other few issues, I am not doing too bad.

I must be doing okay because I have been chosen, along with Martin from the Television Department to represent the store in some kind of sporting event.

Are they mad?

Not about Martin, of course, I have no idea of his sporting prowess, but I certainly know about mine and running is definitely not one of my key capabilities, even if I did have the same size legs to start with.

My legs feature predominantly in my life in general, well they would: I cannot do much without them, however, it is not just because they are odd. When I was younger, we used to go on holiday to a guest house in Blackpool and whilst we were there, we used to go to shows on the pier to watch people like Arthur Askey, Frank Ifield, Kathy Kirby and The Dave Clarke Five. We usually went to shows on the north pier not the central or south ones; Mum had this thing about Blackpool having some less genteel areas and so you stayed in the north. Blackpool was so popular in the 1860s and so great were the crowds of holidaymakers arriving there that a decision was made to extend the Promenade seawards in the form of extra space provided by a pier built at the end of the straight road (Talbot Road) leading to the sea from the railway station. Therefore, in May 1863, north pier was added as an attraction of Blackpool.

At 1,405 feet long, 27 feet wide and built from 12,000 tons of metal it claimed, in its day, to be 'the finest, strongest and most beautiful marine parade in Europe'.

It was advertised as a way of 'walking on water without getting seasick!' The original cost of the pier was £20,000 but another £30,000 was used as ideas developed, that was a lot of money in those days. Opening day was a 'red letter' day for Blackpudlians. Fun-loving spirit overflowed (and so did the pubs apparently).

A town crier greeted people who had been arriving from all over the country since dawn. Some excited, not to mention foolhardy, visitors even dived off the pier in celebration—a good thing that the tide was in at the time!

After three years, a jetty was built extending the pier length to 1,650 feet and two pleasure steamers 'The Queen of the Bay' and 'The Clifton' were bought by the North Pier Company. Visitors in their thousands enjoyed daily cruises to the Lake District, the Isle of Man, Llandudno, Southport and Liverpool. Pleasure cruises from the piers were abandoned altogether in 1939.

In those days, on Blackpool's first pier, the entertainment was very refined and definitely not for the working classes, I think this is why my mum thought it was a bit posh.

When I was only about six, we went to a show in the small theatre on the pier and the compare whoever he was, was doing his 'turn'. He asked for volunteers from the children in the audience to go up and sing a song. My mum and dad persuaded me to go up. My brother was also keen for me to go as well, just in case, they made him go instead.

I was so thin that my legs in a dress used to look like two sticks of celery sticking out of a shopping bag and I was painfully shy. I got on stage with about six or seven other children of various ages and sizes. The compare lined us up and came down the row asking if we would like to sing a song. Some said they would and some said they would not and when he came to me, I just shook my head and did not say a word. The children who were willing to sing performed their nursery rhymes and those of us who did not want to were told it was okay. When everyone had finished, the compare came down the line and gave everyone a stick of rock except me.

Well, I was not going to say anything, because that would be rude. The compare told us to go and we all started to leave the stage, including me, when he then shouted the words that caused my first major embarrassment.

"Oi! Sparrow Legs, where y'goin, didn't y'get one?"

Well, I did not know who this sparrow legs was, but I did know that I had not got a stick of rock, so I turned back. I can clearly remember two big fat old women in the front row in stitches laughing at me, with tears rolling down their faces. I do not know why.

"Have you come with your mum and dad?" He asked.

"Yes, and with my brother," I replied.

"Well, there's a stick of rock for having a mum, one for having a dad and one for having a brother," he said as he laid three sticks of Blackpool rock across my arms. This went on through, how many other brothers and sisters have you got, aunties and uncles, cousins, until I got brave and said, "I'm an aunty." Well, the place was in uproar, I do not know what was funny about that, I have been one since I was five. I ended up with twenty-eight sticks of rock. Oh yes, my brother wanted to be friends with me then.

And that is how I got my first nickname, Sparrow Legs that has stayed with me for years until now.

Not much about my appearance has changed really, I still have a very similar physique. I am only four foot eleven inches, I have not grown very much since those days and I still have very short hair, although it is spiky now, as is the fashion. This hairstyle is another throwback to my childhood, my mum always said, "Short hair makes your face look fatter," nothing to do with the fact that she could not cope with the crying and moaning from me when having my hair brushed. As I weigh just under seven stone, I have kept with that adage and this has earned me my current nickname 'Pete', after the children's character Peter Pan. So, I am not exactly built for running and I have tried to explain this to Mrs Gent.

"Erm I am not very good at running, Mrs Gent," I stated (you have to give people their full titles when speaking to them).

"Well, it is more about the weekend and being recognised for doing well at work," she replied.

"Yes, but I am not good at running," I tried again.

"It's not about the winning, it's about the taking part," she replied.

Oh yes, that is what they always say to people who are absolutely rubbish at any sport and who only get picked in teams because they have friends doing the choosing. Well, I hope this Martin knows what a dud he is getting as a team mate!

The event we are to attend is the House of Fraser Garden Party in London and we have just arrived at our first stop on the weekend itinerary, Greenwich. We have come here to see Gypsy Moth which was the fastest first small vessel to sail around the world and is on display as a memorial to Francis Chichester who has recently died as he was the person who navigated it on that journey. It is situated next to the clipper ship, The Cutty Sark and in the square facing the Cutty Sark pub. I have to say that I think the clipper ship is a lot better to look at than the Gypsy Moth; it is a bit boring really.

I have just had a Babycham stood in the square outside the pub, someone else went inside to buy it and brought it out to me, I still look about five. We are now on our way to the hotel, I have never stayed in a proper hotel before and I am quite nervous and excited all at the same time.

We are staying in The Queens Gate Hotel in South Kensington, it is a grade 2 listed building, I do not know what that means but it is very posh and my mum would be very pleased. I do not think she would be pleased about the bedroom situation though; the bedrooms are nice; it is just that I have to share it with someone else. We have been put into pairs to share a bedroom, I am with a girl from the Henderson's store in Liverpool, she seems very nice but I have never met her before in my life.

We have just all had a sit-down meal around a massive table in the dining room, with white wine and everything. We have been served Escalope Holstein; apparently, it is crisp-fried veal topped with an egg, salty anchovies, and capers. I have no idea what any of those things are but it tastes like steak to me. What with the food and the bedroom sharing, I do not think I will be getting much sleep tonight.

Oh no, Martin may never speak to me again! To be honest, he has not spoken to me much anyway.

We have just finished the race. All the seven girls had to run down the course in one direction and the boys run the same course after baton handover, in the opposite direction, where the girls had just been.

We came sixth. I predictably came last out of the girls and we only moved up the ranks after Martin's heroic efforts on the boy's leg of the race.

Lady Antonia Fraser has presented all the boys with a silk tie and all the girls with a silk scarf, so it is only a pride thing in winning it; I think Martin's pride is a bit dented.

Today is our last day, I am so relieved to get that race over with anything now is a bonus, Martin is still not speaking to me.

We are having a tour of Harrods in Knightsbridge as that is the flagship store for our group. It is amazing, they have got their own chocolate factory which is accessed by going under the main road above and to the other side of the street, I cannot quite get my head around that. They have not given us any chocolates though!

My favourite part of the tour is the Pet Department, I could not believe it when I saw all the animals in the middle of a department store, it is more like a zoo than a shop.

Harrods Pet Kingdom opened in 1917 and does indeed rival London Zoo, apparently you can buy panthers, tigers, camels and baby elephants, although I have not seen any of those today, only dogs and cats and the like, you probably have to order the others. In 1969, Australian backpackers John

Rendall and Anthony Bourke bought a lion cub for two hundred and fifty guineas and kept it in their London flat. I do not know if they have still got it, I should think it will be pretty big by now.

The best kind of people are the ones that come into your life and make you see the sun where you once saw clouds. The people that believe in you so much, you start to believe in you too. The once in a lifetime people.

That is just what I feel like here. They are all like an extra family. All of them call me Pete, well obviously not management and definitely not on the shop floor, and Mr Jones in Despatch resolutely refuses to call me anything other than Vi. It is short for Violet which is not even my name, but most people call me by my nickname, which makes me feel wanted and included.

Oh no, they have gone and done it again.

I am going to be a part of a team of two boys and two girls representing the store in a Sheffield inter store 'It's a Knockout' which is going to be televised on Cable TV.

For goodness' sake, have they learnt nothing from the relay race fiasco?

The real 'It's a Knockout' is broadcast on BBC1. It features teams from a town or city completing tasks in absurd games against each other, sometimes dressed in large rubber suits. The team who gets the most points then goes onto the next stage to compete against another team. You can double your points in a selected round by playing your 'Joker'.

Our version is not as elaborate and consists of the department stores in Sheffield:

- Walshs (us)
- Cole Brothers
- Cockaynes
- Pauldens
- Atkinsons
- Robert Brothers

We are going to be filmed by Sheffield Cablevision. Not everyone has the capability to receive the broadcast unless you live in a council house as the organisation is run by the council. These houses have a cable TV box fitted on a wall, so the occupants can watch the programmes presented.

We have arrived at the City Hall, that is where the tournament is taking place and being filmed, we were told to get here for two o'clock but it appears the games are not going to commence until six. There will be five games in total, I have no idea what they are, none of us do, we will all be in the first game and then, we will all be in a further two games each, each girl with each boy. Each game will have a thirty-minute gap between, so they can sort the cameras out and set the next game up. Work have sent us a packed lunch/tea which we have eaten and the bar opened at five, so we have all had a drink and are dressed in shorts and t-shirts waiting for the games to start.

Oh my god, it is the first game, it is the whole school basketball sports debacle all over again.

The object of the game is to go in turn down the full length of the City Hall dance floor, whilst bouncing a basketball and then when you get to the end, there is a basket attached to a ten-foot pole. You then pick up a six-foot pole onto which you balance the ball and have as many attempts as you need to get the ball in the basket.

Absolute bloody carnage!!

I have bounced the ball once and then kicked it into the audience too many times to count whilst trying to get down the ballroom, starting at the point where I launched the ball into the paying public a yard at a time. I have eventually got down to the basket and have spent the whole game trying to 'shoot' my ball on the end of the pole into the receptacle. Fat chance. If I stood here for the rest of my life, I would not get a single basket; I am too small and I have absolutely no acumen for this game whatsoever! Luckily, the other three players have had more luck and it has to be said, more skill, than me and we are not last.

I need a drink.

Oh, please no, it is the second game and I am in it with Colin Bossington off the Furniture Department and they have only gone and put the joker on it!

This game is like a slalom obstacle course with balloons dangling from high poles ranging down the ballroom. What is it with these people, do they think we are all giants?

The game has started and I am now sat on Colin's shoulders and Colin is subsequently blindfolded whilst he is running blindly, literally, down the course with me screaming directions whilst popping balloons as we career past. OOOOOOhhhhhh, we are winning, Colin is a big strapping lad and I must be at least two stone lighter than any of the other girl participants.

We have won!!! Yay!!! And double points for playing our joker.

The next two rounds have gone well with my other teammates and it is now all on the last game. For goodness' sake, that is me and Matthew of Soft Furnishings. We could win the whole thing if we win this game. No pressure then! It does not help by the fact that we are all as drunk as a skunk as with the bar opening at five and us having a drink in each interval between the rounds, we are a tad slaughtered.

Help! It contains running. And a bed.

The object of the last and let's face it pressurised game is for Matthew and me to run, yes run, up the ballroom carrying a single divan bed. We then have to put the bed down, run back down to the beginning and get covers and pillows, run back up to the bed and make it. We then have to run back down, get a pair of pyjamas each, run back up to the bed, get the pyjamas on and jump into the bed together. Just kill me now!

It is not going well.

Matthew has practically dragged me and the bed up the ballroom, unfortunately, the people of our Bed Department have left the plastic protectors on the base and the mattress. As we have literally dropped the bed onto the floor, the mattress has skidded off the base at breakneck speed and into the unsuspecting crowd.

We have managed to get it back and put it on the base and are hurtling down the other end, well Matthew is, I am just trying my best. Matthew has realised that my best is just not good enough and whilst I am carrying my share of the bedding back up to the bed, he has returned to get both sets of pyjamas whilst I have made the bed. We have both jumped as fast as we can into the pyjamas, a bit of a triumph for me. The other 'big girls' are struggling to get into the men's trouser legs, whereas Peter Pan here has just glided swiftly into them.

We have won the round and we have only gone and won the whole bloody thing!

We are now the proud owners of a magnum of champagne and an engraved metal bucket.

I do not know how that bed is getting back.

Rackham's Department Store 1974

I have just nearly broken my neck on those chuffing stairs!

We are no longer called Walsh's; we have a new name and as a consequence, some of the activity within the store has changed, primarily the eating arrangements for the staff. We used to have three staff rooms/canteens (not that we are common enough to call them canteens of course). One for top management, one for middle management and one for the remainder of us. We now have one big canteen, with a room in the corner for 'management'. This has resulted in the old middle-management staff room being allocated to us on the Lighting Department as an extra stock room.

Floors in Walsh's, now Rackham's:

- Basement
- Lower Ground Floor
- Ground Floor
- First Floor
- Second Floor
- Third Floor
- Fourth Floor

I do not know how much thought went into this allocation because to be perfectly honest it is not very practical. The Lighting Department is on the lower ground floor and our new stockroom is on the fourth floor which is really the sixth floor of the building if you include the basement.

What is wrong with that?

Well, all the floors have a lift to them which facilitates the smooth and easy moving of any stock items, especially bulky, fragile and delicate items like light fittings, however, the sixth floor does not have a lift; it stops, literally, at the fifth floor (known in store as the third floor, very confusing). It is not the easiest activity then to move stock from department to stock room and vice versa. It has been decided that only lampshades will be kept in the sixth-floor stockroom, along with weird things like the plastic make your own lampshades and lumps of liver lamps—they are really called Lava Lamps but we call them the former because that is what they look like.

It is a delicate and tricky activity at the best of times moving the stock around which is my sole responsibility but it is extremely hairy in the three-day week and associated power cuts.

The start of 1974 saw much of UK industry operate under a Three-Day Week restricting their electricity use.

The period of electricity rationing lasted for more than two months and played a pivotal role in unseating the British government.

While the crisis came to a head, thanks to an industrial dispute with coal miners in the midst of a global oil crisis, its true origins date back years or even decades.

In fact, electricity use was rationed just two years before due to fears about potential shortages of coal.

As Britain headed into the 1970s, high inflation led the Conservative Government of the day to impose wage restraint on public sector workers. This sent them headlong into a lengthy and acrimonious dispute with the National Union of Mineworkers (NUM).

Miners picketed at coal-fired power stations, before targeting all other major coal users, including steelworks and ports to ramp up pressure on the government.

With fuel supplies dwindling, the government declared a state of emergency on 9 February, leaving many without power for up to nine hours a day.

We have just had a power cut.

Luckily, we have our own generator but it takes what is probably only a minute or less to kick in. This is good but seems forever when you are in a situation like I am in at the moment; I am halfway down a staircase in the pitch black with multiple lampshades layered up both arms making me resemble a deranged Mexican dancer. Quick, get those lights back on.

December 1974

"Miss, Booth I am seriously disappointed with you, your behaviour last night was not ladylike and you laugh way too loudly," Miss Miller uttered in a disapproving voice.

What I want to say back is, "Well, it wasn't me that had to have my stomach pumped," but what I actually said is, "yes, Miss," like being at school.

Miss Miller narrowed her eyes, turned on her heel and took her considerable bulk to her office hidden behind the Plus Women's Dress Department, quite appropriate really.

That is me told off then, although I do not think it is entirely my fault and I think the store itself should take some responsibility.

Because of the three-day week, sales are down, people do not have the money to spend on luxuries and consequently do not come and shop in the store. Normally, at this time of year, we have a Christmas Party in the Top Rank Nightclub across the road. However, this year, the store have said they cannot afford to do that and the party will be held in the Customer Restaurant, which is normally off limits for us mere mortals.

The party was last night and the alcohol, wine, was provided by the store, from the Food Hall. We no longer have a Food Hall after the arrival of Marks and Spencer on Fargate. I am glad the Food Hall has gone as I hated going down there. I had to go to get boxes to pack the light fittings for customer delivery; it was the obvious place to search. However, the stock room where the empty boxes were kept was down a long thin corridor and of course, I could not just wander in there, I had to ask permission and I just hoped it would be Mr Gunn's day off. But he was more often than not there, lurking. I would ask politely and he would say, I could, then he would follow me very quietly and when I bent over to get a box, he would put his hand through my legs and around to the front and grab my lady bits. He absolutely terrified me but I did not know who to tell about it, so I used to try to find boxes from other areas and avoid him as much as possible.

Well, the Food Hall has gone and thank goodness, him with it but they obviously had some stock left over from when we had the department. It was a very merry night in more ways than one, with lots of wine drunk and apparently me laughing too loud! My unladylike behaviour was when Sharon, of the Frank Usher Department, decided for some reason she needed to pick me up and swing me around the makeshift dancefloor. This was very out of character for Sharon; she is normally very sedate and a bit aloof really and she rarely has anything to do with me, but she suddenly became my best friend and started swirling me around the dance floor, whereupon she fell, me along with her. Two things became very apparent as I got up laughing from the floor, Sharon was drunk and she looked as though she was going to be sick, so myself and Steven of Carpets took her next door into the Hairdressing Department as they had sinks in there.

Once we got there, even though I was squiffy myself, I could see as we sat her on a chair that something was very wrong, she seemed to be unconscious. I left Steven with her as I ran to get help. What happened next was a bit of a blur and as there were so many people in there, I was pushed to the outside of the group. Eventually, someone called an ambulance and went to meet them at the staff entrance and Sharon was whisked away to hospital. I went home at that point.

Sharon is not in work today, obviously recovering from having her stomach pumped and probably alcohol poisoning. The rumour in the store is that the wine was old and had gone off, I do not know about that but I do know that is not all my fault!

Richmond College, Stradbroke 1975

For goodness' sake, what am I like?

Since last year, I have been attending Richmond College on day release, studying the Certificate in Retail Distribution, I am on the second year of a two-year course. If I do well, I will be put forward to go on day release for the higher course, the Diploma in Retail Distribution.

I seem to be getting on like a house on fire. Each year you take four modules and if you pass those with an A, B or C, you move onto the next four modules in the second year. So, I have passed the first year and am part way through the second. It is really weird. I actually understand what they are teaching us and seem to have a natural flair for the subjects. I do not know if this is because I am more settled or that we have all started on the same subject content at the same time. Whatever it is; I am loving it.

I am also enjoying the fact that I am meeting new people and making new friends. I have developed a yearning for the morning coffee break, not because I am desperate for caffeine but it is because with any luck, I will see HIM. Who he? He is the most beautiful man I have ever seen in my life; he looks like a cross between Cat Stevens and Jesus. His name is Zamid and he is from Persia, well I think it is called Iran now; I do not know how I came by this knowledge, but have it, I do. He is attending college full time with two of his compatriots, one who is not much bigger than me and the other who is about six foot six; they make a very striking and exotic trio.

It is strange but I have always tried to be tolerant of other cultures; I do not think that this can be taught; I think it is inherent in your own psyche. It emanates within me from a definite point in my past which if it was a comment on a school report would say 'needs to do better'. The place of enlightenment and the need for me to change was in Oldham Alexandra Park which was a haunt of mine. Apparently, it opened in 1865 and was laid out by operatives who were thrown out of employment owing to the cotton famine in the years previous to that date. The park was terraced, with nooks and crannies and it had a boating lake. It was on this lake that I first met and spoke to my first black person.

Oldham was at the heart of the industrial revolution, and at the turn of the last century, was the centre of the world cotton spinning industry. This, with the associated engineering industry, Ferranti etc. was the basis from which the economy of the town developed. Alongside the hundreds of mills in central Oldham, were the thousands of terraced houses built in the late-nineteenth and early-twentieth centuries to accommodate the mill workers. Between the late 1940s and early 1960s, Oldham, like other parts of the country, received thousands of migrant workers from the New Commonwealth and Pakistan. Earlier migrants were from the Caribbean, followed by people from Pakistan, Kashmir and Bangladesh, and people of Indian origin from East Africa. In Oldham, migrants met the demand for cheap labour in the textile industry, particularly to work on the less popular night shifts. In later years, the migrants, mainly men, were joined by their partners and other dependents. These migrants lived in the remaining terraces that were not knocked down to make way for the new council houses like the ones my uncle and aunty lived in. These boys that I met were the children of some of the Caribbean workers; one was from Jamaica and the other was from Sierra Leone.

I was totally unaware of the politics of the time, especially around migrant workers and in no way was I aware of Enoch Powell, so it is strange that I acted in the way that I did.

John Enoch Powell, politician and classical scholar was born in Strechford, Birmingham on 16 June 1912 and was the only son of two school teacher parents. His mother gave up teaching to bring him up. She taught herself Greek and introduced him to it. He said of his childhood in a house overlooking a railway yard that my childhood was my mother; if I were to design a childhood it would be in the image of mine with my mother. It was his parents who persuaded him not to pursue a career in music.

He won a scholarship to Trinity College, Cambridge, and in his first year, won all the main classical prizes open to undergraduates: this achievement remains unique. His tutor was the poet and classicist A E Houseman. He eventually became a Professor of Greek and Fellow of Trinity College and in 1937, he went to Australia, to the University of Sydney.

Powell is most noted for his denunciation of non-white immigration into Great Britain in the 1960s, a denunciation for which he was promptly sacked from the Conservative Party shadow cabinet by Edward Heath and which caused him to become a kind of non-person in British politics.

"Like the Roman," he told his audience in Birmingham in 1968, "I seem to see 'the River Tiber, foaming with much blood' if immigration into Britain were not checked." The 'rivers of blood' speech became a by-word for 'racism'. Liberal columnist Anthony Lewis muttered in the New York Times that Powell, educated as a classical scholar at

Cambridge, was 'an intellectual who quoted Virgil when he wanted to arouse racial fears'.

I was not aware of these racial fears or these rivers of blood because if I did, I would be quite scared but when the two boys tried to chat me and my friend up, I tried to get away as quick as possible which was pretty difficult since we were sat on the pleasure boat which went round the boating lake at the time. The rest of the afternoon was spent with my friend actively pursuing them and with me pulling away and being very embarrassed. I do not know why I acted like that because I had never heard anyone in my family be racist and it puzzled me deeply even though I could not stop myself doing it. Perhaps, it was the environment around me and I have tried ever since to 'match' my behaviour with my inner feelings of tolerance.

Oh, my goodness, he has asked me out, I am to meet him on Saturday at about two o'clock, at the fish tank in the Hole in the Road. I think at that time of day, we must be going for a coffee somewhere as he does not drink alcohol.

Wrong!

I have just literally had to fight him off.

It is my own fault, I am so naïve; firstly, I have not had many boyfriends and secondly, I am absolutely ignorant of any other ethnicities and cultures, even after the Alexandra Park incident.

We did not go for a coffee but a friend of his, the six-foot-six-man, took us in his car to a house. In my innocence, I just thought we were paying a visit to a friend of theirs, even when he left me on my own in a bedroom and went speaking to someone else in the house did any alarm bells ring. To be honest, I was interested in their language, not that I knew what they were saying, and quite honestly, I was fascinated by a dinner plate lying at the side on a blanket box with the remnants of baked beans on it. I never knew that baked beans would feature in their diet. I immediately got the drift of what was intended when he came back into the room and instantaneously launched a full-scale attack.

We are back in his friend's car now, after nearly having my clothes ripped off me forcibly and he cannot understand what is wrong with me, "I thought you liked me?"

"I do like you," I replied, a little out of breath.

"Well, why did you not want to do it?" He enquired baffled.

"I don't know you," I replied a little high pitched.

"You do," he reasoned, "I see you every week at college."

"I know you do," I answered, a little confused, cudgelling my brain to try and make him understand, "I am not that type of girl."

"Oh," he said as if a light bulb had come on, "you have a boyfriend."

"No, I do not," I practically screamed at him, which was a bit awkward as we had been talking in hushed tones so his friend did not hear, but I suspect he has heard everything though.

"Well, I don't understand what is wrong with you, then," he responded a bit sulkily.

"I am not that kind of girl," I repeated exasperated, pronouncing every syllable, I sound like my dad now.

"Well, I just don't understand," replied Mr Sulky which was quite obvious and I did not have the words to explain. He refused to speak to me for the rest of the journey and unceremoniously dumped me back in town without a goodbye or a backward glance.

Phew, that was a close shave. It is only after I have calmed down and reflected on my eventful afternoon that I realised what had been going on. In his own country, women and girls are closely guarded and have chaperones with them until they are married. Here, because girls are more free and some more promiscuous than myself, he thought he was onto a winner and could not understand why I was not joining in.

Oh dear, Mr six-foot-six-inches obviously heard everything that was happening, understood the state of affairs and has taken it upon himself to intervene in the delicate situation.

I now have a weekly bodyguard that walks me to the bus stop at the end of the day, even though I keep telling him it is not necessary over and over again but to no avail. I will be glad when this academic year is over.

I do not seem to be very good at this 'dating' business, well just boys in general. It all started when I was at junior school in Oldham. I especially loved the Christmas or end of year school parties, you still had the dreaded milk bottles yuk, but this time they were filled with orange juice rather than warm, lumpy milk, much more acceptable. The only problem with the parties was that I was next to the smallest girl in our year, which brought its own trials and tribulations. Jane Taylor was smaller than me, but unlike me, she was very exotic, she went on foreign holidays to Spain. Unheard of. Anyway, I was in no way exotic; I wore boring serviceable clothes, apart from the frilly knickers my mum insisted I wore and my shoes were that serviceable they would be appropriate in the army.

There used to be a game where the girls threw one of their shoes in to a heap on the floor and the boys used to have to get one and match it with a girl, then have the next dance with her. All the girls used to giggle and shriek like girls do and all the boys used to dive headlong at the same time into the shoe pile. I did not stand a chance. It was obvious which my shoe was, mine was the only one that looked indestructible, unlike Jane Taylor's party high heels. I always got Stuart Jones, which was bit of a pain as he was the tallest boy in the year, had ginger hair, always wore short grey flannel trousers and looked, well, dishevelled. Appearance aside, the performance of the Gay Gordons was a logistical nightmare. I performed the whole of the dance on tiptoes at the speed of a runaway train while Stuart was so stooped, he looked like the hunchback of Notre Dame.

Now, if I could have danced with John Fellows, well, that would have been heaven. He was gorgeous; Jane Taylor probably danced with him and all the other popular boys.

It is obvious to me that I have always had trouble with my appearance; I did understand that I could not change my physique, I was skinny, still am and that was that and I knew I could not do anything about my odd legs. My mum had taken me to physiotherapy when I was little but that did not work, I just used to cry and moan all the time I was there, so she stopped taking me. But there was one facet of my appearance that I could change, my hair, you could grow your hair. Well, you could if you did not live with my mum.

I so wanted long hair. Jane Taylor had high heels AND long hair; Janet Baines had high heels AND long hair, I had flat shoes and short straight hair. I must have worn my mum down a bit because I remember on one occasion, she gave in and let me grow it. It could not have grown that long because I cannot remember any photographs of my childhood with my hair any longer than short! I suppose I was my own worst enemy because when my mum used to do my hair in the morning when I was growing it, I would cry. Perhaps, she pulled it just that little bit harder because she thought long hair made my face look thinner. It was always that same response, "Short hair makes your face look fatter."

"White tights make your legs look fatter."

The fateful day arrived. I came walking out of school totally unaware of what was awaiting me. It was my mum. I was at junior school for God's sake, your mum does not come to collect you, but worse was yet to come. "I've made you an appointment and we have to go now," she explained.

"An appointment for what?" I enquired.

"To have your hair cut."

So, that was that. I was led to the hairdressers like a sheep to the slaughter and I cried for hours all the way through the appointment and even when I got home. It could not have been very nice for the hairdresser, but to be honest, I was not bothered. I was back to the beatnik look.

My mum made another hair appointment for me I recall when I was about eleven, to have my hair permed.

"Curly hair will make your face look fatter," she explained.

Mum could not come to the hairdressers with me for some reason probably because she thought I was old enough to go on my own; so she sent me off with a letter in my hand detailing what the hairdresser should do to my hair. It was a different salon than before, perhaps Mum thought I was too traumatised with the memories to return to the old one. There were only two people who worked at this hairdresser, the main stylist and the junior, and they were both men, very unusual.

This then was my first encounter with unrequited love, well apart from Mark Winter who was on the telly on a Saturday night after wrestling, but that did not count. It was also the start of my unnatural long-term longing for Tizer.

I was in the salon for hours, children were normally in and out quickly if they went at all, it was much cheaper for your dad to perform the styling in front of the fire. Other children though did not normally have perms, bit out of dads' league that, but no here I was with Kirby grips everywhere. But all my reservations melted away when I saw the junior. I did not mind being sat with curlers in my hair for hours on end. The problem was it was quite a hot day and I was getting thirsty, I suppose they thought they could not offer me a cup of tea but luckily, the junior had bought a large bottle of Tizer but he did not like it.

"Would you like a drink?" The stylist enquired.

"Yes, please," I replied adoringly to the junior. He could have given me a glass of sludge and I would have drunk it; I was totally besotted with him. Fizzy pop was a great treat for me in any case, occasionally, if we were lucky me and my brother had a bottle off the Corona van that came around. Our favourites were Limeade and Cherryade.

The stylist realised my adoration and seemed to find it very amusing; I thought it was because he was just teasing the junior. It was not until years later that I realised that I had not got a cat in hells chance, the fact that he was too old for me was not the problem, he was gay. At the time, it did not matter because I had not got a clue what that meant other than being happy. The only disappointment of that day as far as I was concerned is that I left the salon looking like a bizarre throwback to the early 1950s. I had a fifty-five-year old's hair style on an eleven-year-old head and the junior did not even let me take the empty Tizer bottle back to the corner shop and claim the penny back.

Well, I was very concerned about this three times a bridesmaid thing. Of course, I had had John Rushton as a boyfriend but that was when I was seven. I was thirteen, surely, I should have a boyfriend by now. I did not know what was wrong with me, I spent hours in front of the mirror trying to get the Colgate ring of confidence. I never found it.

Perhaps, I had the wrong self-image, what I felt I was inside did not really match with what was on the outside. I could never have been accused of having a quiet disposition and I have to admit, I always had something to say for myself. This maybe where the problem lay because I was convinced that I was Marina, Aqua Marina from Stingray. Marina as well as being a puppet it has to be said, was a tail-less mermaid from an underwater continent. She had been rescued by Troy and Phones from Titan, again all puppets. Marina was mute and she had been sworn to silence by Titan telling her that it she spoke again, her people and her city would be destroyed. Marina was passionately in love with Troy. Well, I thought I was Marina, the romance of it all was too much, the angst of not being able to tell Troy how much she loved him and being relegated to just flapping her arms at him. And, the fact that Troy was in love with her too and used to sing that song to her:

Marina, Aqua Marina,

What are these strange enchantments that start whenever you're near?
Marina, Aqua Marina,
Why can't you whisper the words my heart is longing to hear.

You're magic to me.
A beautiful mystery,
I'm certain to fall I know,
Because you enthral me so.
Marina, Aqua Marina,
Why don't you say,
That you'll always stay,
Close to my heart.

I was Marina!

I had had a sort of a boyfriend though. Me and my friend from the Albion Pub had met these boys Gary and Martin that lived near Byron Street. They both lived in semi-detached houses, very posh and Gary had omelettes for his tea. I had never in my life heard of an omelette, never mind seen an omelette before but his mum kindly showed me how to make one. I never did try it at home; I do not think my dad would have liked it. Gary's dad worked in some sort of steel or engineering works and he made us all a ring with our names punched into the front. I had to have 'Viv' on mine of course because Vivienne was too big to fit on it. Gary was my friend's boyfriend and they seemed to be getting on well snogging and all that, but I had snogged that Martin once and I was not snogging him again, I did not like him.

These previous childhood liaisons, if you can call them that, have had an impact on me and I have obviously still got the same issues with choosing the wrong boys to go out with.

Rackham's Department Store, 1976

They have only gone and done it again, why do they keep asking me and more to the point why do I keep saying, Yes?

There is to be an Inter-Store Sports Day at Stocksbridge Sports Centre and I along with four other girls are going to represent Rackham's in the Women's Five a Side Football Tournament.

What?

I know nothing about playing football, let alone the longstanding, excuse the pun, usual leg issue, it must be because we won the It's a Knockout.

In the team are two girls I do not really know plus little Lydia from the Fashion Department; she is even smaller than I am, which is going some, Susan from the Stationery Department and me. For some reason, I cannot fathom, when they must know my sporting acumen is zilch and even less around football, they have decided I am going to be the person who kicks off for our team.

What?

Lydia, Susan and myself have arrived at the Sports Centre, we did have a bit of hairy moment when Lydia's husband who was driving us to the event calmly informed us as we were driving down a steep hill that his brakes had failed. However, we have all arrived here in one piece and our chauffeur has retreated to get his car fixed.

We have changed into white t-shirts and shorts, which are the 'colours' for our store, other activities are being played in matching attire by other Rackham's employees. We have met up with the other two girls on the indoor tennis court which is today doubling as a football pitch. We are 'pitted' against the team from Marks and Spencer and the winners of this match progress onto the next round. We had no chance! For a start, they are all big burly girls and they obviously know how to play football. They have beaten us 5-0 which is a miracle it is not a bigger score; I suppose it is because you only play for a short time in five a side. Thank goodness. We are battered and bruised because apart from them being burly, they are also dirty players and I have been laid flat out on the floor more times than I wish to remember.

Lydia, Susan and myself are now sat in the ladies' changing room contemplating our injuries; the other two girls have changed and gone home.

"I know what is good for injuries," Lydia exclaimed, "soaking in water."

"Yes, well we haven't got any water. Have we?" I questioned.

"Yes, we have," she stated triumphantly, whilst Susan and I gaped at her open mouthed, before both asking simultaneously, "Where?"

"The swimming baths," she replied in a *are you two daft manner*.

"They are swimming races in it," I screeched.

"Not the big pool, the kids' pool, which no one is using," she responded, as both Susan and I absorbed the information whereupon Susan said, "Good idea, but we haven't brought any swimming gear."

"I have thought about that," replied Mrs Know-all, "we can take our underwear off and go in the pool in our shorts and t-shirts."

We did not really think it through, we both immediately thought it was a brilliant idea and got changed into just our t-shirts and shorts. It was a little challenging getting through the main swimming pool arena without causing too much inquisitiveness but we have managed it and have all three jumped into the, at the moment, completely empty kids pool.

We have been swimming around quite happily, keeping the noise to a minimum when a group of men and boys from the men's Rackham's five-a-side football team have appeared around the pool, ball in hand. They have just thrown the ball to Lydia to which she has jumped up triumphantly to catch it.

Oh, my god.

I have to explain our physiques at this time, Susan has a very lithe figure that goes in and out at all the right places; I am as is well documented tiny and have nothing in any of the places; Lydia on the other hand may only be four foot ten inches tall but she has enormous boobs. These bosoms are now on display to all and sundry because to our chagrin, we have now realised too late what happens to white material when it is wet through.

We have just spent the last thirty minutes sat on the pool steps, with just our heads sticking out of the water, with our arms folded firmly across our breasts.

The men have finally given up and gone.

We now have the issue of getting through a full auditorium of swimmers and audience into the safety of the changing rooms whilst appearing to any casual onlooker as three fully naked females.

The decision has been made, we are going to get out of the kids' pool and run as quickly and as quietly as we can into the changing rooms. Well, that is ok for them, it is that word, *run* again!

We have made it across the auditorium and into the changing room in a sort of crocodile formation, Susan first, me second and Lydia bringing up the rear. Once reaching safety, we have gone into whoops of laughter; Susan and I are hugging each other partly to keep ourselves upright and from falling over through a fit of the giggles engulfing us and partly through relief.

Where is Lydia?

We have just realised that Lydia is not with us, she was definitely behind us when we left the kids' pool and as we ran nakedly across the auditorium but is nowhere to be seen in the changing rooms.

She has just come darting in red-faced and beside herself with laughter.

"Where have you been?" We both exclaimed together.

"I ran in the men's changing room by mistake," she spluttered.

Blame Is a Clever Trickster

Rackham's Department Store 1977

I am very excited.

I am sat in Personnel waiting to see Miss Fanshaw in her office, Mrs Gent has long gone, retiring to a cottage in Torquay. I have just returned from a holiday and I am going in to see her to get my results from college as I was not here when they were published.

I still continue to do well. I completed and passed my second year of Certificate in Distribution Management and consequently was put forward to do the first year of the higher qualification, Diploma in Distribution Management. I have not had to deal with the previous issue of an overzealous Iranian bodyguard as they have all returned to their own country.

I was also put forward for the Sale Assistant of the Year through the Chamber of Commerce; I had my picture in the paper and everything. I did not win it; I came second. The photographer from the newspaper said to me that it was not won on good looks. Well, that is a bit of a back-handed compliment if you ask me seeing as the winner was a rather rotund boy from Cole Brothers.

There are only three of us on this higher course from Rackham's Steven from the Carpet Department, Carol from the Hosiery Department and me. There were four subjects in the first year of the two-year course, again with an A, B or C pass. If any of us do not achieve that in one subject, we will be allowed to take the second year, resisting the failed subject as well as the next four areas of study. If we fail more than one subject, then that is it; we cannot go further.

Oh, she is ready for me, I am going in.

"Good morning, Miss Booth," is the greeting.

"Good morning, Miss Fanshaw," no first names here, I do not even know what her first name is.

"I have your results here and I am afraid it is bad news, you have failed two subjects and so you will not be able to advance to the second year," she stated.

I do not know what to say back, I am so disappointed and a bit confused really because all my work over the year had very good marks and I thought I had done really well in the exams. Plus, she has not even asked me if I have had a nice holiday.

"Erm, I know you said I have failed but can I have the results anyway please?" I asked a bit crestfallen I have to say.

"I am sorry, Miss Booth, but I do not have the actual grades in front of me," she responded.

Oh!

"Could you tell me please then which subjects I failed in?" I persisted. I am not normally this forward but I really wanted to know.

"No, I am sorry I do not have that information, thank you for your time, Miss Booth," she replied dismissively, and we both knew that was my signal to get up and leave which I did after thanking her. I was so excited and now I feel like the wind has been taken right out of my sails.

I should not have done it; I should be down in my own department, but I am on the Hosiery Department discussing the situation with Carol.

"I have just found out I have failed two subjects and I am not allowed to carry on," I blurted out at breakneck speed; we will be in trouble if we are seen 'gossiping' on the shop floor.

"Oh, I am sorry," she replied. "I'm not going next year either, I have failed one subject and should really be able to carry on, but as Miss Fanshaw said, I have just got married and may want to start a family and that would be a waste of money for the company as I would leave."

I have heard through the grapevine that Steven failed two subjects, but they are allowing him to re-sit those and carry on with next year.

Sheffield December 1978

I have no idea how I am going to get home from work, it was bad enough coming this morning. When I looked out of the window at about eight o'clock, I thought it had been raining very hard as the ground looked wet.

Oh, my god!

As I walked up the drive, I realised it was not water on the floor but black ice and somehow managed through the performance of a triple salchow not to slide bum first back down the drive but to wrap myself around the telegraph pole at the top. This is how my next-door neighbour found me on his way to work. He managed to free me and set me onto level, if very slippery ground and said that he would give me a lift to work, which was very kind of him but in hindsight, not a very bright idea on my part seeing how is vehicle is a Robin Reliant.

Anyway, I made it here in one piece but now I have got to try and get home after it has snowed heavily all day on the black ice.

We are in the middle of the Winter of Discontent, which is characterised by widespread strikes by private and public sector trade unions demanding pay rises greater than the limits Prime Minister James Callaghan and his Labour Party government have been imposing. These disputes have caused great public inconvenience, exacerbated by it being the coldest winter for sixteen years and severe storms have isolated many remote areas of the country.

Everything has been made worse here in Sheffield today because the gritters have gone on strike and so the roads are untreated. The store has decided to close early because the staff need to get home and there are abandoned cars littered all over the place and the buses of course cannot run, so everyone needs to walk to their respective abodes.

Arnold who works on the Men's Clothing Department has just come to find me and suggested we walk home together, he lives on the next road to me, good idea. He of course is prepared for the day, has studied the weather forecast and the political situation and is dressed appropriately for the conditions, I on the other hand am not. I have got my big coat on but, my footwear although not high heels are closed in wedge shoes, so are not ideal for the weather.

We have left the staff entrance and around the store, which has gone okay, probably because it is undercover and so slightly sheltered from the elements. This is not the case as we traverse High Street and Fargate. I have slipped twice accompanied by manoeuvres an acrobat would be proud of and have managed to keep upright, whilst screeching and 'ooooohing' like a demented pigeon, however, at the top of The Moor, I have been lulled into a false sense of security whilst passing under a shop awning and this time, my acumen for acrobatics has let me down and I have slipped flat on my back, accompanied by the screeching, oooohing and also now a fit of giggles. Arnold has hauled me back onto my feet and said for the third time, "Vivienne, will you PLEASE get hold of my arm!"

I am not holding his arm. I do not want to be rude; he must be twenty years older than me; he coughs constantly, his chest goes in instead of out and he has a dewdrop on the end of his nose permanently and if he thinks I will be seen in public linking him, he has another think coming. I do not want anyone to think he is my boyfriend.

This slipping, sliding, falling and giggling on my part has continued down The Moor and subsequently on two-thirds of Abbeydale Road, with Arnold chastising me and telling me to get hold of his arm, which I keep flatly refusing.

We have managed to reach Abbeydale Cinema in this manner and have been met with a bit of an impasse; there are cars strewn everywhere with people trying to push them into the side near the pavements rather than leaving them in the middle of the road. The snow at this juncture seems to be packed more solidly and therefore a lot more icy and slippery and I have gone down once again. Arnold has now lost his temper with me slightly and said exasperated, "I have had enough of this now, you have been on the floor more times than you have been stood up, get hold of my arm now."

I have uttered a muted, "Okay," and have done as I have been told.

We now have to traverse the road whilst manoeuvring around a car stuck in the middle of the thoroughfare at an angle, being pushed by several burly men. As we cannot go around the back, we are walking in front of it, so they have stopped pushing it to let us past. Unfortunately, at this point, I have lost my footing again and as I am holding on to Arnold's arm, I have taken his legs from underneath him and both of us have landed spread-eagled on the bonnet of the car.

Arnold will not hold my arm anymore and I have had to walk the rest of the way unaided, needless to say I have been on the floor several more times.

House of Fraser Department Store May 1980

Oh, my god, it is staff training morning and I am late.

Bloody buses! If you time it wrong, you either get a bus that gets you to work too early, one that is just on-time or one that is really late, sounds like the three bears. It all centres around a specific minute in the morning which calculates your arrival time and displays no logic at all.

I am rushing up to the Haberdashery Department as fast as my little legs will take me and Ernie, the joiner, is fiddling about with something near the top of the escalator and is looking at me with a strange expression on his face.

What is the matter with him?

Oh, shit it is Miss Brian.

Miss Brian is in charge of the Ground Floor and is a bit of a formidable woman; there are a few of those types here and they all appear to be spinsters of a certain age. Apparently, she is having an affair with the assistant store manager, I do not know about that, seems very unlikely to me; they are both a bit boring and extremely old. Just as she reaches the top of the escalator, I am frantically trying to get up, Ernie says with great authority (which is very unusual for him as he is a quiet bloke and quite frankly, not his place as he works down in the basement), "Don't you dare run up this escalator in your condition, you take your time, no matter who is glaring at you!"

That was very brave of him and very sweet, he is of course referring to my condition, I am six months pregnant with my first child.

This speech seems to have some effect on both myself and Miss Brian; I slow my pace in deference to Ernie sticking up for me and Miss Brian seems to have tempered what she was likely going to say to me and utters authoritatively and a little accusingly, "Miss Booth, your staff are awaiting you."

I have been married for ages now and she still calls me 'Miss'.

House of Fraser Department Store June 1980

For goodness' sake! Do I have a sign on my head saying 'Weirdos this way?'

It does not bode well for my last week working for House of Fraser, I am leaving on Friday after seven years of working here to have my first child and be a housewife. I got promoted to Assistant Buyer on the Suits Department (ladies of course) a few years ago, I did try for the Haberdashery Department initially but did not get that job but they gave me Suits instead. Jane got the appointment working for Miss Brian, I may have scuppered my chances when I could not reply correctly to the question of whether I knew what a French seam was. Well, I did not but I did ask what it was which resulted in Miss Brian showing me one in her own skirt which she had constructed thereby giving me a view of her underwear. I might be wrong but I think that incident may have had some bearing on the outcome.

I loved working on the Suits Department but then Miss Brian got the Ground Floor Manager job, Jane was promoted to Buyer and then I was asked to do the Haberdashery Assistant Buyer Role.

I wish I was on Suits now because I do not think this would have been happening up there.

"Do you have a pink hairbrush for sale please?" The polite but definitely scary man enquired.

I think I have responded immediately although it may not be so as I have been looking around wildly for some kind of help in my current situation.

"No sorry, we don't sell hairbrushes on Haberdashery, they may have some on the Cosmetics Department though," I believe I have replied calmly, although I may be wrong and I really do think I need to phone security as soon as I can get rid of him.

"But I want a pink hairbrush," he wailed.

Yes, and I want you to pull your flaming pants up is what I thought but I replied again, "As I said before, we do not sell them on this department."

For goodness' sake, he just keeps staring at me from the other side of the counter, with his trousers just resting on what I believe to be a very excited penis, and I have to say he has a profusely hairy pubic area. I am really trying not to look in that direction but I am finding it very difficult and my eyes seem to be drawn there as if by some invisible magnet.

It is no good, he will not go; I am just going to have to ring them and try and be discreet and not startle him as I have no idea how he is going to react when he hears me asking for help in regards to him.

I have rung the security number, it is ringing and someone has answered, "Hello."

"Oh, hello, this is the Haberdashery Department and I have a little bit of a situation," I did not want to say my name because I did not want Mr Erect to know it and also, I did not want to trigger any other activity.

"Yes, we know," she replied, "we are watching you; we are just waiting for his trousers to go a little bit lower and then we will have him for indecent exposure."

Oh cheers, thanks for that!

Sheffield Friday 2 January 1981

At ten to eleven tonight, Peter Sutcliffe was arrested in Melbourne Avenue, Sheffield by PC Robert Hydes. He was with prostitute Miss Olivia Reivers. Both were taken to Hammerton Road Police Station in Walkley for questioning.

Saturday 3 January 1981

Sergeant Ring returned to Melbourne Avenue and found an engineer's ball pein hammer and wooden handed knife.

Sunday 4 January 1981

Peter Sutcliffe admits he is the Yorkshire Ripper.

May 22 1981

Peter Sutcliffe, the serial killer, The Yorkshire Ripper was found guilty of murdering thirteen women and attempting to murder seven others between 1975 and 1980.

The women in Sheffield had lived in fear through those five years, even though The Yorkshire Ripper targeted prostitutes, no one felt safe. My friend Kate and me decided we should learn self-defence, Jujitsu at the YMCA, the fact that the building is situated right in the middle of The Yorkshire Ripper's stomping ground did not seem to figure in the decision. We chose that site because it was near Sheffield University where my friend Kate went and on Friday nights after we had our lesson 'The Student Union Night' was on just up the road; again this was right in the middle of the area of where the prostitutes were.

The idea was good in itself to learn self-defence, the actual way we dealt with the lessons was not so good.

When we got there, we had to do a warm up which consisted of fifty sits up—predictably I was rubbish, it was almost impossible because my little leg seemed to have a mind of its own and would rise off the floor at any opportunity. This resulted in the lady teacher having to sit on both my feet to enable me to participate. Once this was eventually achieved, we had to all kneel down equally spaced around the judo mat and then we had to place our forehead on the floor whilst chanting something. I never knew what the chant was because as soon as my forehead hit the mat, I would be consumed immediately by a massive fit of the giggles.

The lesson itself was not much better, not any fault of the teachers, they did try to teach us appropriate moves. One successful move for me was if someone tried to strangle you from behind, you moved your neck into the crook of their arm and then threw them over your shoulder, because I am so small, I was brilliant at that move and people seemed to literally fall over me. I was also good at the break falls which are designed to be utilised to avoid injury, who would have thought that having one leg shorter than the other would have been an advantage in that situation. The problem was everything else. One example that is very clear in my head is when they tried to teach us arm locks. It was not so much when I did an arm lock on someone else, it was when they did one on me. If a move hurt you to get out of it, you were to tap your leg or arm or floor or whatever; my inborn reaction was to scream, unfortunately, this was not a sign for people to let go. I would be screaming so much that I forgot the tapping and it would take my friend Kate saying, "Her face is going very red," to make my combatant release me.

Once the lesson was over, we would go to the ladies' toilets to get changed, put our makeup on and get dolled up for the university event. We would have brought with us a large bottle of cider and a four pack of Babycham, we drank two of the bottles each and half the bottle of cider each whilst getting ready. Once we got to the venue, we would drink about three pints of cider each; at the end of the evening, we would walk home through the red-light district towards home in the middle of the night. How we thought two drunken women with limited experience in self-defence would repel a serial killer, I have no idea. However, the lessons did come in handy at the university event itself.

I had a white t-shirt and lace top that had no back to it and sort of tied at the back at my waist. This meant two things, I had a bare back and secondly, I could not wear a bra. It was not see-through at the front but it was quite obvious around the nipple area that I was not wearing a bra and so I utilised two pieces of Sellotape. In hindsight, I really was asking for trouble. We had an unwritten rule that if anyone asked us to dance, we would have one dance with them even if we did not like them because that was polite and we did not want to hurt anyone's feelings. We would have the dance and then make our excuses and return to each other. So, a guy asked me to dance, I did not really like him, but as was our rule, I went to dance with him and then went to go back to Kate who was at the bar; he was not happy and tried very hard to keep me where I was. He was slightly aggressive but I managed to return to Kate intact if a little flustered. His friend who he had attended with was waiting at the bar near Kate, so he went to stand with him and I stood with Kate. He was directly behind me and he kept nudging me in my bare back and I was getting just a bit fed up with him after the earlier issue. I would turn around each time and glare at him, tell him to stop, turn back to Kate saying, "If he carries on, I am going to hit him."

Kate looked back at me with that 'yes of course, you are, I've heard this all before' expression on her face and so it continued two or three times more. At this point, I think he felt he should up the ante and proceeded to pour his nearly full pint of beer down my back and so into my trousers and knickers.

I do not think he was expecting what happened next, I know Kate definitely did not and to be perfectly honest, even I was a bit shocked. I spun around and punched him full on his nose. After a stunned second, he came to his senses and moved forward and said, "I'm sorry," whereupon I kicked him with all my might on one of his shins and turned round to look at Kate. I was furious, but the look of sheer horror on Kate's face just set me off into whoops of laughter, and my tormentor and his friend made a hasty retreat.

I seemed somehow to be attracted to the Ripper's area of activity in Sheffield, later on when me and my husband first married before we bought our own house, we nearly rented a flat in Melbourne Avenue but a bigger flat became available on Ecclesall Road which we took but that was only just over a mile away from Melbourne Avenue anyway.

I always seem to be in the wrong place at the wrong time. There have been two major serial killer episodes in the last twenty years and somehow, I seem to be involved with them in some small way. However, someone must be watching over me because the other incident I was in was a similar but scarier situation in Oldham when I was eight years old.

"No," we all cried incredulously in unison.

"Yes," Susan Gow replied authoritatively.

"Noooooooo! I don't believe you!"

We were all sat in Susan Gow's front room after her birthday party, she was nine or ten I think, I was still eight and was the baby of the class and did I know it. We were all staring at Susan with our mouths wide open.

"Shut y'gob there's a bus comin'," someone giggled nervously.

"Give over, I'm bobborin m'self," someone else whispered amid shouts of 'Shut up!' and 'Charmin!'

Susan had been telling us about the Moor's Murders. Not that we called them that, we did not call them anything we just talked about them in some kind of fascinated horror and decided what they did and did not do, very sensationally it had to be said. We had not a clue really as to what actually went on. We were by now sat in the dark all cuddled up Susan's front room carpet in front of her gas fire which I thought was very posh because we had a coal fire at that time.

Twenty-eight-year old Ian Brady and twenty-four-year old Myra Hindley were a murderous combination of personalities. At a young age, Brady burgled houses, that was what got him his first time in prison. At prison, he learnt all he could about the outside criminal world and decided he would be an enemy to society there and then. Brady and Hindley first met while they were working at the same office. They talked of their sadistic tastes and showed the same interests in Nazism and pornography. It was then that they became a couple, not a nice thought.

In September of 1964, Brady and Hindley moved in with Hindley's grandmother. It was at this time Brady was introduced to Myra's sister, Maureen, and her seventeen-year-old husband, David Smith. Brady immediately wanted to impress Smith with his tales of thieving and criminal knowledge and to prove himself more to Smith, Brady picked up seventeen-year-old homosexual Edward Evans, on 6 October 1965. Brady tied Evans up in his home and then invited Smith over, when Smith went over, he was invited in and Brady then smashed Evan's skull in with an axe in front of Smith who was horrified but he did not want to let Brady know, so he said nothing and went home.

The next day, Smith contacted the police who arrested Brady and Hindley. The police searched the house and found the dead boy in the bathroom and also found evidence of other murders. With this evidence, the police then dug up the Moors north of Manchester and discovered the bodies of two children. Brady and Hindley's modus operandi was to pick up young people, sometimes the poor victim was subjected to rape and mutilation, then killed and buried. It was estimated that they killed about six young people.

Ian Brady and Myra Hindley were convicted of murder on 6 May 1966 and sentenced to life imprisonment.

We knew none of this detail, all we knew was that there was a man and a woman on the Moors near Indian Head killing children. We did not really know that was where it was happening, we just thought it was and believed that it was and to be honest, it was more like folklore rather than the truth to us, like a ghost story passed down from years ago. I had not seen anything on the news about it but it has to be said that I never watched the news, it was only on at certain times of the day anyway. We only had two channels, BBC1 and ITV at home because you needed a different aerial for BBC2 and we did not have one. Which I have to say was a bit of a pain because when my friends used to go on and on about Alias Smith and Jones and how gorgeous Pete Duel was or Ben Murphy was, I had not got a clue what they were talking about and could not join in even though I tried, just for appearance sake, you understand. I did not want everyone to know I could not watch it; it was more like I felt like I was missing out on something.

As far as newspapers went, I never saw anything about Brady and Hindley, probably because I never read a newspaper ever. We did have newspapers in the house, we had the 'Oldham Chronicle' in the week and 'The Green Un or the Pink Un' on a Saturday. Me and my brother did have 'Dandy' and 'Beano' once a week, well they were my brother's really and I got 'Jackie' when I was a bit older but that did not really help. In fact, magazines and not knowing what was going on led me to have a very embarrassing moment in the first year at junior school.

Miss Lee was our teacher, she was probably in her twenties, had short blonde curly hair and long spiky finger nails. I remember those finger nails well, she used to jab you in your arm with them to every syllable when she was mad with you, which seemed very often I have to say. I did not like her, she was scary. It was Art. We had to design the front of a women's magazine. Well, I had a slight problem here, I had not got a clue what she was taking about. I sat for quite a long time doing nothing and I knew if I remained like that the jab of a nail was coming my way, so I plucked up courage to ask and put my hand up.

"Yes, Vivienne, what's the matter," she enquired deceptively sweetly. We all knew that voice.

"Miss, I don't know what a magazine front looks like."

There were sniggers in the class and a few looks of incredulity directed at me, "Don't be silly, Vivienne, of course, you do," she spat as she turned away.

Well, she might think I did but I did not I thought indignantly. My mum did not get magazines; she sometimes got a copy of 'Family Album' off Mrs Denson but that was it. I sat there for a while pretending to do something and then came to a decision, well, I would just have to copy. That did not work either. I got into so much more trouble for copying off Pamela Wood than I did for asking what a woman's magazine was. What was I supposed to do?

As far as Brady and Hindley were concerned, all the adults around us were well aware of what was happening and so much so, which is why I got in trouble on Asia Field.

Asia field got its name because it was a piece of land behind the Asia Mill and was the nearest thing to a field around where we lived. To get to it from my house, you had to walk down Drury Lane, under the railway bridge and turn left. There was a ginnel that went by the side of the railway embankment and round the back of the garages on Glebe Street. Glebe Street was a dead-end road with a row of terraces which faced the front of the Asia Cotton Mill and where the main entrance to the mill was. Down the side of the entrance was a wide path that led to Asia Field. At the back of the mill was the lodge of water.

Practically, every mill in Oldham had a lodge or small dam of water whose purpose was to condense the steam from the mill engines. The problem was that these lodges became the natural surface drainage of the town. In 1880, the waste water including the contents of the toilets and slaughterhouse offal went into the mill lodges. That does not happen now but it still looked very murky. To the right-hand side of the lodge on the far end of Asia Mill was the back of The Emmanuel Church where my sisters both got married. Through the middle of the field ran a little brook, which was in reality part of a sewer I think but it was the nearest thing to a stream near where I lived. At the far end of Asia Field was a main road which was where the Ferranti Mill sat.

We were always on the field when we were a bit older, I suppose because it was the only bit of green land around and about. We would play 'house' especially in the ruins of the pigsty which was a bit hazardous I have to say because it was always surrounded by nettles in the summer, but it was not too bad because there were always loads of dock leaves around. When I say they were ruins, it was really only the footings of the buildings that were left. There were many scattered about but we tended to keep near the pigsty. How we know that it was a pigsty I do not know.

On a sunny summer evening, me and Janet Dudley had decided we wanted to find my brother for some reason, I do not why but we did. We also decided for some reason unbeknown to us that he was on Asia Field, so we would go and have a look. We were not frightened of being on the field at night. It was about a quarter to eight but we did not want to walk down the passage at that time even though we were not frightened, so we approached the field down the side of The Emmanuel.

It was quite obvious that my brother was not on the field but we thought we would have a walk down to the brook anyway while we were there. The brook started about a quarter of the way down the hill, just to the side of the piece of land where my brother and his friends gave me the bumps. As we walked down the dirt path, a man that my dad knew came walking up with his dog, the dog was brown and ginger and all fluffy, we tried to fuss the dog but he would not have any of it. The man did not speak, he just nodded to us and walked pass. As we approached the brook from our side, we could see another man on the other side just near the 'bumps' patch. We did not really take much notice of him; I just remember he was wearing a leather jacket and had slicked back hair; I think he was a rocker. We were stood on the brow of the hill when the man with the dog came back and said,

"Come with me, I'm going to tell your dad about this."

Me and Janet just looked at him in fascination but we decided we should do what he said as he was an adult and walked behind him and his dog, we just kept looking at each other in amazement. What had we done? The man did not even live near the field, he lived down near Turf Lane and he had come back to get us and takes us to my dad. We were baffled. We were even more confused when we got home and my dad sent Janet home and me into the house when the man said, "I found them wondering around on Asia Field with some strange bloke near them."

When my dad came in, he did not say a word to me and acted as if nothing had happened. How could we have been in so much trouble to be marched off the field but not get told off?

I am convinced the man was Ian Brady.

Asda Supermarket 1986

You would have thought that I would learn, but obviously not because I am currently crouched down hiding under a supermarket checkout.

After I had left House of Fraser, I had my first daughter Jessie in August 1980 and subsequently my second daughter Daphne in September 1983. I have been doing the hardest job in the world for six years, being a mother, but I have not gone out to work until now. I love my kids to pieces but it has come to a point that I need something else in my life, something to at least stimulate my brain a bit and let us be honest, we could do with the money. The thought of my returning to work though has not been accepted completely by all the family, there are those that would prefer me to stay at home waiting patiently for them to return in the evening and be so grateful they did! So, erm, no that is not going to happen, things need to change.

I applied for a checkout assistant job a few months ago, I do not have any daytime childcare, so working evenings and a Saturday afternoon in a supermarket was the best option. They did not have any positions available when I applied and they said they would put me on a list and if any became available, they would let me know, and they have.

Why am I hiding under the checkout?

We have been taught that when typing in the cost of any bottle, pop, wine, beer etc. to lay the bottle down so that it does not inadvertently fall over the side of the checkout bed, which I always do religiously. However, today, that strategy has let me down enormously. It is the whole pea situation again. A very nice older couple have visited my checkout with their shopping and have a significant number of large fizzy pop bottles which I have laid down flat, as taught, as I have checked them in. Unfortunately, as I sent the last bottle down the checkout bed, the bottom of it has hit the top of one already down there and all hell has broken loose. The lower bottle, ginger ale, has exploded and has sent the contents at high speed out of the bottle and straight into the face of the unsuspecting gentleman customer. He has cleverly tried to employ avoidance tactics by stepping from side to side to try and avoid the jet stream, but the bottle is very astute and seems to know instinctively in which direction he is going to go and is therefore following him precisely. During this activity, which seems ages, which was probably only a moment I have been screeching loudly whilst chasing the writhing bottle unsuccessfully at first with it alluding capture with it eventually running out of steam, and ginger ale and so I have managed to grab it. As I have looked up, the poor man is absolutely soaked with ginger ale running down his face and glasses. I have done my best to apologise and even though a young customer on a checkout further down has gone into whoops, I have persevered with a straight concerned face. I am afraid my resolve has left me when his wife said in answer to what seemed like my hundredth apology, "Oh, don't worry, love, his jacket needed a wash anyway."

Well, that has done it, I have looked at the lady, her husband and the whooping customer and I have gone into a complete fit of the giggles and I am hiding under my checkout because I cannot stop and if I continue to behave in this manner there will be more than ginger ale to mop up.

Asda December 1990

Oh, my god, I have just asked for a Page Three topless model to come to Customer Services.

Not that we have a topless model working here but we have a lady called Samantha Smith who works on the Clothing Department, she is a nice-looking lady but I do not believe, she models as a side line. I have just asked for her over the public address system for her to come to deal with an item that has been returned, but for some reason I asked for Samantha Fox.

Well, apart from a very indignant Clothing Department representative and some extremely amused colleagues, I have had to deal with an inordinate amount of young men who have just appeared as if by magic at Customer Services.

I have come back to work at Asda after having a short amount of time off to have my third daughter Jemima in June. Money is tight for everyone and especially in this area of Handsworth where Asda is based. It is just up the road from the coking plant at Orgreave. In June 1984, there was a violent confrontation, known as 'The Battle of Orgreave' between miners picketing the plant and officers of South Yorkshire Police. It was a pivotal event in the 1984–1985 UK miner's strike and one of the most violent clashes in British industrial history. Historian Tristram Hunt has described the confrontation as "almost medieval in its choreography… at various stages a siege, a battle, a chase, a rout and finally, a brutal example of legalised state violence."

Seventy-one picketer were charged with riot and twenty-four with violent disorders. The trials of the men collapsed when evidence given by the police was deemed 'unreliable'. The repercussions of this event are still felt today in local society, both socially and legally as negotiations continue for compensation.

I do actually prefer to work on Customers Services even though it is for the majority of time dealing with complaints and returns. I have to say that I really do not like working on the checkouts which I still do as well, interspersed with Customer Services. I also work on the newspaper counter which means in addition I also have the customer counting responsibility; this entails walking around the store every thirty minutes, clipboard in hand, counting the number of customers at predetermined locations around the supermarket. There are some very lovely customers but there are those who presume that you are stupid because you are a checkout assistant and that therefore you do not have a brain. It could of course be that I have massive chip on both of my shoulders around people thinking that I am less than intelligent.

Due to my childhood education being severely disrupted, my Diploma in Distribution Management being stopped before it really began and living with someone who constantly tells me that I am stupid, I have decided to do something about it.

I am taking a Mensa test! I did one by post and they have invited me to take a supervised test at Jessops Hospital in the centre of Sheffield. Talk about feel out of place. There are about ten of us invited to do the test, a dad and his young daughter, a couple of middle-aged women, a few bearded men and me. I am the only one wearing makeup and definitely the only one with dangly/sparkly earrings on.

Mensa is the largest and oldest IQ society in the world. It is a non-profit organisation open to people who score on the 98th percentile or higher on a standardised, supervised IQ or other approved intelligence test.

Mensa use two IQ tests—Culture Fair where a score of 132 places a candidate in the top two percent of the population. On the Cattell B III test, a score of 148 or above is required to be a member.

Oh, my god I have been invited to be a member of Mensa! The IQ test I have taken is the Cattell B III and I have scored an IQ of 151, which is in the highly gifted section. ME! Who would have thought it?

I have not been to any of the meetings though as the feedback seems to suggest they just constantly discuss how to get a Gnu on the top deck of a double-decker bus and other such conundrums. I have got a gold Mensa card though.

Being a member of Mensa, although 'poking a snout' at certain people and proving a point to myself if no one else, is not going to be recognised as a valid qualification in progressing my career away from Asda. I have decided to take my Maths and English GCSEs at Handsworth Community Centre, seeing how I failed so miserably at those subjects in my youth. There is a creche which have accepted Jemima with open arms and I am doing both qualifications in a year rather than the normal two. My idea is to get those under my belt and then try to go to university and study a Business Studies Degree next year as I believe I missed the chance this year. In the meantime, whilst studying my GCSEs, I have applied to Richmond College to try and find out the results of my first year of the Diploma of Distribution Management. Once I have them, I will try and study the two subjects I failed in the year after completing my GCSEs and whilst waiting to apply for university. It has cost me ten pounds which is a lot of money for me, but it will be worth it.

The bloody bastards!

I have just received the results from Richmond College; I passed all four subjects with flying colours, two As and two Bs. I might be wrong, but I do not think that I am, that Steven from the Carpet Department pinched my funding because he is a man and I am not!

Sheffield Hallam University 1993

Year One

I actually feel physically sick.

This is my first day on a Business Studies BA(Hons) part-time five-year degree course, which is from one o'clock to nine o'clock every Thursday afternoon and evening. The interview process was bad enough but actually coming into the building and going into a class is one of scariest things I have ever done. I have managed to get on the course a year earlier, but it is a week after all classes started, so not only am I a 'mature' student without the required five GCSEs (I have three French C, I passed at sixteen and Maths B and English A I passed this year). I am already behind before I have even started.

The head of the course who interviewed me last week said extremely candidly to a very red faced, sweaty me, "You have not got the required qualifications needed by a mature student to join this course, but I believe you have the potential."

Well, I will bloody need it because here I am a week late and doing Computer Studies as my first subject. Of course, they do not call it that, it has a posh name, but it is learning how to use Supercalc spreadsheets and DB4 databases. They might as well be talking a foreign language to me because I have no idea what any of that means. Also, I have never used a computer in my life, making sure the kids have food, clothes and the odd treat is my objective, electronic equipment has never figured in those goals. I am sat here in embarrassed mortification because I do not even know how to turn the damn thing on. Oh, a nice lady on the course who works for the university has shown me what to do, thank goodness, this does not bode well.

Who would have believed it I have only gone and passed the first year, even the IT module—oh module, see I am even talking like a university mature student now.

Royal Mail IT 1993

"Put her down, she's new!"

This was shouted as some random man who physically picked me up and ran down the street with me, with my new colleague chasing us both in hot pursuit.

Can you actually believe it?

I have only gone and got a job in Royal Mail IT, me! How ironic I could not even switch a computer on this time last year. I am on the Helpline and working on a new barcode scanning system for Registered and Recorded Mail. I just cannot get my head around it; I have taken to it like knife through butter.

It has not been plain sailing to be sure. Jemina is still only four and is not at school yet, just nursery and although the other two are at school, this post is full time and so cover is needed in the morning, evenings and school holidays. As I do not have any child care, I have had to have a childminder and therefore more than two-thirds of my wage each month goes to that lady. It will be worth it in the end to get my foot in the door and start on a career I did not know I even wanted, never mind any acumen for it. This has caused a massive issue, because there is someone who firstly does not want me to go out to work and mix with other people and who is also extremely unhappy that I am embarking on the career that they desire.

Year Two 1994

I have completed the first trimester of the second year and am halfway through the second trimester and I have had to stop for the moment. I have had an on-going health issue since the birth of my last daughter and I have to go into hospital for a hysterectomy. Ironically, it is the same hospital as I had my Mensa test.

Jessops Hospital for Women was built in 1878, it was commissioned by Thomas Jessop, a wealthy steelworks owner when he made a donation of twenty-six thousand pounds to build it, which was a great deal of money in those days.

For, goodness' sake, if that woman does not shut up, I might have to go outside and have a word with her myself. I am currently on a ladies' ward after my operation and sleep is difficult enough without her caterwauling outside.

What is not stated in any description of the hospital is that it is located in the red-light district of Sheffield, facing a church and graveyard on one side of the building. Very convenient, a women's hospital, church and yes there is a pub, maybe the hospital was placed there on purpose.

My ward is on that side of the building, it is four o'clock in the morning and all I can hear is a woman shouting, "Work it, work it, work it."

Investigation has revealed by my looking out of the large Victorian window next to my bed, two women and a man. The first female is loudly shouting those words and the other female is what can only be described as crouching astride the man who is laid reposed on top of a gravestone while she is relieving him. I have to say none of them look anything like Julia Roberts or Richard Gere!

Royal Mail IT 1995

I am just so nervous, you would think it would get easier, but it has not. However, I do not think he thought it through properly, by telling me just as I am walking in the door to start the interview that the panel do not want me and they wanted someone else had quite the opposite effect I expect than he was intending. I do not know why as a senior work colleague, he felt he needed to tell me that just as I was going in.

I have worked on the Helpline and then moved into the development area of Royal Mail IT and the job I am being interviewed for is within the consulting arm of the business. If I get it, my grade will go up by three steps and my wages by seventy percent, so 'Mr I am trying to put you off' has just made me all the more determined.

Oh, I know two of the board but I do not know the third, but I definitely know him by reputation. He has introduced himself, Tommy Shanklin, and then remained quiet whilst watching me answer a couple of questions and has now decided to join the fray.

"Do you mind if I read out a section of your application letter?" He has enquired sweetly; you are not fooling me, mate.

"Yes, of course," I have replied in the same manner.

"It says here that you are an excellent team worker but that you are quite able when required to work on your own initiative," he read calmly, "is that correct?"

"Yes, it is," I replied again in the same manner as him.

"You are a right, clever little devil, aren't you?" Came the thrust.

Immediately and without hesitation I laughed at him and responded, "Yes, you could say that."

He has now reverted to his silent, observing approach as the other two ask me further less contentious questions, oh he is back again for a second go, "It says on your CV that you are in the process of taking an Honours Degree in Business Studies," stated the snake. "Is that correct?"

"Yes, it is," I replied awaiting the next parry and here it is. "What has taken you so long to try and get some decent qualifications?"

I looked him straight in the eye and said without a moment's hesitation and without a hint of emotion, "I lost both my parents when I was young just before my O levels and was as you can imagine traumatised and so I have now started back on the education path."

I have got the job—witwoo!

Royal Mail IT 1996

When did life get so complicated?

I am now a single mother of three children.

Year Three 1997

What is his chuffing problem?

I think it must be because I challenged his authority. We have just started taking International Business as a module in the third year of the degree. I did well to get to this point, even though I had missed several months and taking my exams in November with the resits instead of June with the others. I had to have a whole separate date for my French module, but I passed my second year, yay!

This man has already been reported by some of the females on the course for a very chauvinist comment he made; he said that he preferred the view of women that his colleagues had that he worked with in the oil industry in the Middle East. We could not believe it when he went onto to say that first there are men, then there are cattle, then there are insects and then there are women! The authorities have done nothing about it, even though quite a few of the women present complained, he is still with us.

He had asked a question for us to research for the following week, which was 'which currency is the best when doing business travel in Europe'. As luck would have it, Royal Mail does quite a lot of work for The British Postal Consultancy abroad, research in discussion with the consultants that perform that work says that they are always sent with American Dollars when in Europe. So, that was the answer I gave him and he is just not happy. He told the class that the currency is Euros and when I explained why I had given that answer he got even shirtier with me. So, that must be it, he is annoyed with me and definitely does not like me.

We have just done a presentation, two men and two women, one of them me, and have each had to speak for a couple of minutes around points within the subject matter. I went as red as a beetroot, I am just not used to public speaking, but I got through it. He has then critiqued each of us in turn, saying what we did well and highlighting areas that needed improving and he has just got to me and said, "And, you, I don't what it is that you do, I can't determine it, but somehow it seems to work."

Charming!

It is not all academic fervour; it is hard work but it is fun too. As we are mature students and have jobs etc., we are studying part time and so do not get the same experience that we would have if we had left school and then gone to university. There are no halls of residence, partying all night, cheap beer at the uni dances on a Friday night. However, there are occasions when we do have a bit of a laugh.

We are currently sat in The Howard Pub just across the road from Dyson House where we attend our four Thursday lectures. The reason we are in the pub is because the second and the third lectures have been cancelled which means we have a free period of four and a half hours, including the break between the afternoon and the evening sessions.

We are not all here, most of the men are here along with me, the only woman; the other ladies have taken the sensible option and have decided to spend the hours productively doing course work.

But no, here I am getting drunker by the minute and have come to realise that there is no way I am going to make the final lecture at seven thirty, and neither is anyone else here going to either. As can happen in these situations of copious alcohol consumption on an empty stomach, we have wandered onto a subject of discussion which would not normally feature in polite conversation—strippers. When I say 'we' have meandered into this debate, there are two exceptions, myself and Graham who are not participating. I say Graham, he may be called Graham or he could be called Duncan, I have no idea which is his correct title. It is not as though I do not know him, I have been on the course with him for six months and we are great friends but I just cannot call him by his correct name, even if I knew which one it was. He does not seem to mind and answers to either of them.

Being excluded from the discussion has not rendered us deaf, we can hear quite clearly what is being said, and are both sat here with differing expressions on our faces. I myself am displaying what I should imagine is an 'interested' look on my face, although I suspect with the amount of alcohol that I have drunk, it is probably coming across as a leer. Duncan/Graham on the other hand has got an expression on his that is very easy to determine and describe—disgust.

I have just leant over to him and whispered, although I am not sure at what volume I am speaking, the question, "Would you go and see a stripper?"

"I would rather rip my liver out with a rusty coat hanger," came the response.

Phare and Away

Bratislava, Slovakia December 1999

First Day

Can I get to Birmingham Airport from Chesterfield in one hour and thirty minutes?

I have just stepped out of the shower to hear the phone ring, Colin from BPCS (British Postal Consultancy Service) has just asked me this question. Might be a bit of a push seeing as how I do not drive, but Mr C is up for a challenge and off we go. Good job, I have already packed my suitcase and have got my passport and original travel documents with me. These documents however, are no longer valid, let us hope we can get to the airport in time and the new up-to-date papers.

What I have not told my husband Mr C, is the rest of the conversation, if I had I do not think we would be travelling at breakneck speed down the motorway.

I am off to do a piece of work in Slovakia to look at a computer system they have in their Post Office for key customers and then design a new and much improved system which can be accessed by the users to run reports rather than them keep having to ask the IT department to run them causing a lot of delay and cost. Once I have got the requirements, designed and produced the system, it is then going to be rolled out to Post Offices in Slovakia, Bulgaria, Albania, Slovenia and Macedonia through a European Union project—no pressure then!

What I have not told Mr C from the telephone conversation is that I am supposed to fly from Birmingham to Dusseldorf and then on to Vienna (Slovakia does not have an airport access from the west, so I have to fly into Austria). I am then to meet Burt at Vienna Airport, who also works for BPCS on the customer side, who will then convey me to our hotel.

Wrong.

It turns out that my flight to Dusseldorf has been cancelled and I now have to fly to Frankfurt instead. As the timings are different when I arrive in Vienna, Burt will be in a meeting and will not be able to drive the forty miles over the border to collect me. I have to get a taxi in Vienna, Burt has helpfully given me the name of a firm at the airport, and then travel to The Hotel Devlin in Bratislava on my own. All I know is that the hotel is on the Danube—that is one big river.

Phew! We have made it with fifteen minutes to spare, Colin had spoken to the check-in desk and they had kept it open for me. I have made a quick 'goodbye' with Mr C as a fire alarm has just gone off and he has had to evacuate and I have been ushered into departures and onto the plane, blimey.

I have never been to Frankfurt before, well, I suppose I have not been there now as I am only in the airport. I have just caused a bit of a stir to be honest. I have never been to this airport before, in fact, I have never travelled abroad on my own ever and have just got a little bit lost. I have never had to do a transfer from one plane to another and I will admit, I got a bit disorientated and confused but have now found the correct departure gate for Vienna, and I have joined the group of people for passport checks.

The man on the border control has just looked at my passport and then looked at me a little perplexed and said, "You are not Norwegian?"

What?

"No, I am not," I have replied as equally perplexed. He is looking at my passport which clearly says I am British, and why would he think I was from Norway? I am a short, slightly dumpy, dark-haired woman and in all my imaginings have I ever thought, I look the least bit Scandinavian. Plus, we are in Germany.

"But you are not Norwegian," he repeated.

What is wrong with him? It is quite clear I am not and that my passport is British.

"No, I am not," I have repeated, this conversation may take some time if we are just going to keep repeating the same things over and over again to each other.

"Then, why are you with all these people from Norway?" He said with a 'ah, ah' attitude.

I think he might be a bit strange.

The penny has just dropped, as I joined the queue late, these are not the people transferring from England but from Norway.

Once we have established that I do not indeed need to be Norwegian to board this plane, I have been allowed on and have taken my seat for the journey to Vienna.

I have arrived at the airport in Vienna and found the booth for the taxi firm Burt has recommended and have paid my taxi fare for the forty-mile journey to Bratislava. The people in the booth speak English, unfortunately my taxi driver only speaks German and I only speak English and limited French and neither of us speak Slovakian.

This is going to be interesting.

From what I can gather, he does not know the whereabouts precisely of the Hotel Devlin just the general area. Well, I think that is what we have discussed and with a shrug of his shoulders, we have set off on our journey. *'The taxi is very plush, a Mercedes, I think, with leather seats and everything, it is already dark outside.'*

We have left the city and are travelling through the Austrian countryside; it all looks very pretty with houses dotted around at some distance from each other. All seem to be displaying outdoor Christmas lights, seems a bit early in the month for this, not the twelve days before Christmas Day and twelve days after, but each to their own.

I have just had a bit of a panic attack. Here, I am a woman on her own in a car with a man I have never met before in my life, in the pitch black, neither of us know each other's language and we both have no idea of the language of the country we are traversing to. It is a good job I did not tell Mr C what I was going to do.

I can see some lights, it appears to be the border control between Austria and Slovakia, there is a big long queue of cars waiting to have their documents checked.

Oh, my god!

He is jumping the queue and is driving alongside the stationary cars towards Passport Control. It is a good job I cannot speak German or Slovakian because by the look of the hand gestures they are all making to us, what they are saying is not very nice.

Good grief!

There are border control guards pointing their rifles and guns at us. Mr C will definitely not be happy about this.

Wait a minute. They have let us through, phew!

The rest of the journey has gone on without incident and we have arrived on the outskirts of Bratislava. My driver is now using body language which is depicting a search for the hotel; he is also speaking but I do not have a clue what he is saying but I presume it is about the exploration for the desired destination. To show that I am on the same page and understanding what we are doing, I have moved forward on my chair and am sat in the middle of the back seat with my head poked forward in the space between the driver and passenger seat.

"There," I shouted with triumph, and I have pointed my finger in the direction of a big blue neon site somewhere in the distance displaying the words 'Hotel Devlin'.

My driver has acknowledged the trajectory of my finger and is trying to negotiate the one-way system to get me to my destination. He has failed. He has stopped the car and has uttered the one word he knows in English 'Out'.

I am now stood in a bus station, in a foreign country, the taxi has left and it is nine o' clock at night. All you can hear are the clip clopping of my heels on the pavement as I try not to run, there do not seem to be many people here, which is good news but I am very wary of the dark shadows in the corners of the bus shelters.

Thank goodness, I am at the reception of the hotel.

I have checked in and have made my way to the bar area as instructed by Burt, I am to meet him there with Jaroslav, the Marketing Director of the Post Office in Slovakia to discuss the plans for tomorrow. Colin must have given Burt a good description of me because whom I presumed to be Burt has just stood up and is walking towards me with his hand held outstretched. I suspect he has recognised me not because of a description but because I stick out like a sore thumb in this environment and am the only unaccompanied female in the bar other than the 'ladies of the night' sat in a corner.

We have made arrangements for tomorrow. Jaroslav has gone home to his family and I am on my way to my room for a well-earned sleep and a bit of a calm down. Burt is going to stay in the bar for a nightcap but not before he has had to first accompany me in the lift to my room as the rest of the men in the hotel have decided I am 'fair game' as I am a woman on her own.

Second Day

My brain hurts.

I am exhausted, it is one thing to try and determine someone's system requirements at home but is a whole new ball game in a foreign county, never mind that the computers have a Cyrillic keyboard. Thank goodness, Jaroslav speaks good English or else I think my part in this project would be destined for failure.

For light relief after the heavy morning, Burt has suggested we do a bit of sight-seeing.

We have just visited Cumil, the sewer worker. He is not a real person obviously but a bronze sculpture of a man peeping out of a pretend manhole with just his head and shoulders sticking out. Apparently, it was installed in 1977 in an effort to spice up the look and feel of the area, however, Burt has another version, he thinks the statue of the man is one of the revolutionaries who used the sewer system to outwit the opposition. I do not know which version is true all I know is he is very easy to trip over and I imagine there has been many a drunken person caught out by this bronze peeping tom.

I have just bought a souvenir pottery lady ornament off the Christmas Market. I have never been to a Christmas Market before, so I have no reference point as to whether this is good or bad. All I know is that my own lady statue cost one hundred and twenty Slovak Korona which I think is about two English pounds. Another 'first' for me—I am drinking a cup of hot mulled wine; you pay for the cup and get that amount of money back when you hand the receptacle back to the vendor—it tastes very nice.

I think the mulled wine must have acted as some sort of relaxant on me as otherwise I think I would be freaking out.

We have just crossed the road at some traffic lights, when the crossing light is on green of course as otherwise we may be fined for jaywalking, and are walking down a narrow street in the midst of a crowd of people. We definitely look out of place and can be quite easily identified as 'tourists', not just because of our clothes and demeanour but also because we make such an odd couple visually. Burt is six feet four and I am just five feet at a push if I stand on my tiptoes.

Oh, my word, what is happening?

A group of about five men have picked up what looks like a barrier you have for crowd control when there is a state visit or a royal wedding or something and are running towards me carrying it. They are acting like sheepdogs where their instinct is to get around their prey and draw their targets together as a bunch. However, these are trying to cut me out from the pack, which they have done and have now pinned me by the barrier against a brick wall. I have no idea where Burt is and the road crossing crowd seem to have dissipated as if by magic.

Ah, Ah! That did not work then!

This is obviously an opportune crime, which I believe they must have practised before if the disappearing multitude are anything to go by, they obviously know the signs of what is going to happen. One of the 'herders', which one I do not know as it has all happened so quick has tried to get into my handbag and steal whatever he can. Well, I have outwitted him, not physically on my part as I am still wedged against a wall with a dirty great big barrier across my chest, but by foresight. I have brought a handbag with me where the tag that controls the zip has fallen off thus making entry into the receptacle at speed impossible. All of sudden, all of the herders have run away and I can see Burt.

What a day.

"Where do you want to eat tonight?" Burt has enquired sometime later as we are sat in the bar at the hotel.

"Erm, I don't know, why don't we eat in the hotel?" I replied a little warily.

"I don't think the food is very good," came the reply.

I do not care, they are not going to pin me up against a wall with a dirty great big barrier in here is what I wanted to say but responded, "Well, you know Bratislava better than me, so wherever you think."

I think my face must have given away my thoughts, "Are you worried about what happened this afternoon?" He questioned, followed by, "Don't worry, we can run."

Oh yes, mate, you can run; you are six feet four with big long legs. I am five feet, with one leg shorter than the other!

I have been as jittery as a tap-dancing spider at her first dance recital on the way to the Chinese restaurant, but we are here and are seated ordering our meal. When working for BPCS, you are allowed certain expenses for your stays away from home and as part of your evening meal, you are permitted the cost half a bottle of wine. As there are two of us, we can purchase a full bottle. I always drink white wine, but being the 'novice' traveller in this relationship, I have let Burt chose the wine, he has ordered a Cabinet Sauvignon. Oh dear, I really do not like red wine.

Wrong! This is lovely.

Third Day

"Can you stay another night away but in Vienna?" Cathy from BPCS queries. "The thing is if you go home on Sunday, the cost of the flight will be a thousand pounds less than you going back on Saturday."

"Yes, yes," I replied. "That's fine." Who would not want to spend an all-expenses paid night in Vienna? Even if I am on my own.

"You can pick whichever hotel you want because the cost of a night in a five-star hotel will be nowhere near the cost of the flight," she ended.

I am stood outside The Austria Trend Hotel Europa Wien directly facing St Stephens Cathedral, Stephansplatz. Burt has just dropped me off in a taxi and he has continued on his way to catch his flight home. I have made it back to Vienna with no 'incidents' at Border Control this time.

I have checked in and have found my way around, sort of and have stumbled across a Christmas Market and have bought a cup of mulled wine, getting quite good at this market lark now. This time though, it is in a paper cup, so you do not have to do the deposit thing and so I am getting a little bit over-confident to be honest and have bought another cup. I have only had a coffee and a piece of cake today, this purchased in a small cafe the acquisition achieved by me through a lot of pointing. I have to say I am feeling very mellow now.

I am wandering around looking in shop windows wondering what to do with myself. I would love to go for a spin in one of the horse and carriages that are parked around the cathedral, but I am just not confident enough to do the transactional stuff involved, so I roaming around at a bit of a loss. Oh wow, a brass band have just struck up and people are following them around Stephansplatz. I have joined them, mulled wine in hand and I probably should not be dancing as I am, but hey ho, this is good fun.

I have decided not to eat in the hotel tonight because I feel very conspicuous and extremely self-conscious, so I am going to go out and try and find somewhere to eat. After the Bratislava episode, I do not know if this is brave or downright stupid. I have had a brainwave—they have a TGIs in Vienna, they are bound to speak English, and they do but that is where the helpfulness has stopped.

"Can I have a table for one please?" I have enquired of the front of house waitress.

"One?" Has come the response.

"Yes, one please," I repeated.

"One?" She questioned.

"Yes, one." Oh, here we go again, she is going to ask me if I am Norwegian in a minute.

"We don't have tables for one," she replied looking at me with a 'don't you know anything look'.

"Well, there is only me." So there! I answered looking around the restaurant. I have realised it is full of family groups, a lot of whom I must admit are staring curiously at me.

My very tall blond waitress has indicated that I should follow her with a flick of her lovely hair and a bit of a huff. She has sat me at a table where she has removed one of the chairs and the remaining chair is facing a brick wall, with another wall to my right abutting the table and a staircase to my left. I have started to giggle. I feel like I have been told off and I have been put in the naughty corner, I have no idea what is going on in the rest of the restaurant behind me. I think ordering lots of beer is the answer to this.

Sofia, Bulgaria March 2000

First Day

I have done the preliminary design of the system and have arrived at Hotel Maria Louisa in Sofia, Bulgaria.

Burt is already here and tomorrow we are going to the office at the Bulgarian Post Office to meet Roslana who is in charge of the project here and her assistant Bengi who is going to translate what I have produced in English into Bulgarian.

This hotel is a bit strange; there seems to be only myself and Burt staying here; well, there is only us here having breakfast, maybe we are early or late, I do not know. The only other people I have seen are the staff and some very burly men sat on chairs outside the doors of some of the bedrooms. I have not eaten much, I am a bit nervous and do not know what to expect today, also I have a bit of a 'phobia' about eating in front of people I do not know. It is as if Burt has been reading my thoughts because he has just said, "We won't be eating lunch today. Last time I came, they took me to the canteen and we had cold beetroot soup and cabbage. It was disgusting."

Thank goodness for that, we both obviously feel the same but for different reasons.

I have met Roslana and Bengi, they are lovely. Roslana is single and Bengi is married with a little boy and they both speak excellent English. We have had a very productive morning and Roslana has just enquired, "Would you like to have some lunch?"

I do not know if it is the panic on my face or the look of disgust on Burt's but she has laughed out loud and said, "Oh no, not here, in a restaurant." So, we are off out.

This is a bit of a shock. We have left the Post Office building and are walking to the restaurant, the road is full of pot holes and the pavements are even worse, it will be a miracle if I can keep upright. All around us are derelict bits of land, abutted on both sides of the road by massive, soulless blocks of flats and what seems to be hundreds of dogs just roaming around. Roslana has explained that when the communists came, they banned people from having pets, so the dogs were just left on the streets.

We have arrived at the restaurant, to call it that is a bit too grand. It is a great big shed facing a couple of random shops, a tobacconist and what looks to be some sort of toy/hardware shop, both are closed as it is lunch. As we enter into the restaurant, to the left is a sort of bar and an enormous semicircle open fire/oven and there are rows of trestle tables and benches along both walls. We have selected a table and bench and are looking at the menu.

Oh, my god.

You can have soup or omelette, soft drinks or beer. Roslana and Burt are going to have beer, I have opted for Coca Cola as I have a heavy afternoon ahead and I think my senses are already overwrought without the addition of alcohol. I just do not know what to have. Roslana is having potato soup and Burt is having an omelette. I do not know how well they will cook the omelettes; I hate snotty eggs and I do not want potato soup; the only other option is chicken soup and so I have opted for that.

What has been brought to me looks nothing like any chicken soup I have ever seen before and is in a receptacle resembling a washing up bowl. I cannot really see the contents as the very watery liquid has a green, greasy scum on top.

Oh no.

I have started to attempt to eat it and have put my spoon in and apart from the green water I have located a noodle, that is it, nothing else. The next spoonful has revealed the same liquid and a thin piece of carrot and the best bit in the next spoonful, a bone bereft of chicken. Roslana is paying for our meal, and I know they are not very well paid, so there is no way I am not going to eat it. I will have some bread to soak it up that will help.

Wrong!

This bread is awful, it is so dry and seems to have the knack of getting stuck in the back of my throat.

Second Day

We decided last night to eat at the hotel, thank goodness. It was a buffet style meal and so I could pick and choose what and how much I ate but my stomach was still seriously indignant when I finally went to bed.

How sweet is that?

I have just sat down at my designated desk in The Bulgarian Post Office where I left my laptop yesterday ready for work today. Draped across it is what looks like two pieces of red and white wool fashioned into some sort of figures.

It is a Martenitsa. These are normally given to people in Bulgaria on 1st March or 'Baba Marta Day' as it is known. It is said that Baba Marta was a grumpy old lady whose moods changed like the March weather, from sunny to rainy and so forth. It is a small piece of adornment made of red and white yarn, usually in the form of a white male and red female.

Ah, that is what it is. Apparently, you wear it until you first see a stork, swallow or blossoming tree—I think it will be a swallow or tree I will see first, I do not think they have storks in deepest Chesterfield.

I was not here on 1st March but Roslana and Benji have decided to give it to me today, 8th March as they are also celebrating Mother's Day in Bulgaria (it is always on this day, different than the UK where it moves around to land on a Sunday) along with International Women's Day. There have been lots of ladies popping in and out of the office all morning and just as many phone calls all celebrating both events. It is very strange but I have noticed that all the 'top' jobs here seem to be performed by women and the men involved in the company sit in the foyer smoking and waiting to ferry people around. Another thing you can smoke wherever you want in this building, the Marketing Director, another lady, smokes like a chimney all day long in her office. I know this is a massive generalisation and may just be in this industry, but that is my observation, the gender bit not the smoking.

We are off for lunch.

Oh no!

It is the same menu and if they think I am having that chicken soup, they can think again. Roslana and Burt are having beers and omelettes, I have opted for Coca Cola and potato soup, it definitely looked a lot better than the chicken yesterday, who could believe that would be the case?

Roslana has returned from ordering and has informed me that they did not have potato soup today so she has ordered me the chicken soup as she saw that I liked that yesterday. Give me strength.

After another heavy work day and a lot of complaining from my stomach, we have ventured out into Sofia to find somewhere to eat for our evening meal. We have not succeeded. To be honest, it all seems to be a bit intimidating. There are so many people begging, trying to sell you shoelaces, weigh you or clean your shoes. These poor souls are not frightening, in fact, I have nearly been in tears looking at a little four-year-old boy covered in bruises trying to sell us shoelaces but it is the menacing men waiting in the shadows ready to pounce to take the money that are truly scary. Even Burt seems worried as the night is drawing in and so we are going back to the hotel to eat.

Whilst we were out and about, we saw a man dripping in gold as the saying goes, I can clearly see where that description comes from when looking at said gentleman. Although I think he is no gentleman. He is followed around everywhere by his entourage, the self-same burly men I have seen sat outside the bedrooms in our hotel. As we have been wandering around looking for somewhere to eat, they have all been going in and out of the other hotels we have passed in Sofia. We have ordered our meal in the hotel restaurant and the golden man has now arrived in a flurry of activity in the restaurant in our hotel and has sat down for his meal at a table next to us. The attentiveness from all around him is extraordinary.

Third Day

I have nearly ascertained all the additional information I require from Roslana and especially Benji to go with the initial material I got from Jaroslav ready to 'tweak' the system ready for the 'launch' in June.

We are now off to lunch.

Not again!

Burt has gone to order this time, Roslana and Burt have gone for omelette and beers as usual and I have given in and gone with an omelette too. I do not care if it has snotty eggs, my stomach cannot take another chicken soup and I have gone for beer as well.

He has only gone and got me a bloody chicken soup!

He thought I liked it and had forgotten I wanted an omelette as I had had soup for the past two days. For goodness' sake!

I really do not think my stomach is going to recover from this visit as Roslana has just produced something that looks distinctly like sausage rolls from under her desk. Apparently, they are not sausage rolls, they are Banitsa. Banitsa is a traditional pastry dish made in Bulgaria, North Macedonia and Serbia. It is made by layering a mixture of whisked eggs, natural yoghurt and pieces of white brined cheese between filo pastry and then baked in the oven.

Roslana felt that as it was our last day in Sofia before returning to the UK that we should have something special to eat in the afternoon and she had spent all of last evening preparing and making these delicacies.

Oh no! There is no way I cannot eat them; I just hope my stomach forgives me.

Bulgaria June 2000

First Day

Blimey, it is warm. I did not expect it to be so hot in June in Sofia—fool that I am. I may have brought the wrong clothing.

Today has gone well, the BPCS lot are here with the participating country representatives arriving tomorrow. The presentation of the system has gone well but I just need to 'tweak' it a bit to fit the screens provided as part of the project. It appears that apart from different keyboards, they have got different specifications for the screens. Hey ho! May be a long night.

Second Day

Sorted.

The delegates from the participating countries have arrived, Slovenia has decided to back out of the project because of political reasons—blimey and the Macedonian representative will arrive later to have a private meeting with me—sounds a bit ominous.

Roslana and Benji are here, along with Jaroslav from Slovakia, these I already know and feel as though they are already firm friends. Mr Kurti (I have no idea of his first name) is here from Albania, he is some 'bigwig' in the post office there and is the ugliest man I have ever met in my life, he seems to like me though. He does not speak any English and so has brought along his interpreter, Albana, who seems really sweet. Colin from BPCS is also attending, along with Burt who has brought with him his wife Rose and another gentleman whom I have never met before called Len. Len is in his late sixties, similar to Burt and is from Norfolk; he is the first person I have ever met that speaks like Mr C. The main focus for Len is not the actual project, he is totally consumed by the colour of Albana's hair, which he is not a fan of and will tell you so at numerous occasions throughout the day.

That went very well, off to meet Slobodan from Macedonia.

Oh, my god!

He is one scary person.

To say he is an antagonistic is an understatement. Firstly, he is from the IT gang who wants control over all systems and so does not want to relinquish power to the minions but more importantly, I am a woman asking him to do so. Well telling him actually.

We are off into town in a fleet of taxis to have a meal together at a Bulgarian restaurant in the centre of Sofia. I am in a taxi with Colin, Burt, Len and Rose, I am squished in the middle of the back seat.

Oh, my goodness! We have just passed the football stadium where fans on a previous occasion celebrating fired live ammunition into the air and killed some poor woman who had wandered onto her balcony for some evening air. I think it is the stadium, we are driving so fast and erratically, I do not really know.

Thank God, we are here, that taxi driver is a mad man.

I am sat with Mr Kurti and Albana in the restaurant. Mr Kurti has taken a shine to me and keeps calling me Pretty Woman or Miss Vivienne from the film; I think there is something wrong with his eyesight, never in my wildest dreams have I ever thought I look like Julia Roberts.

I have ordered a traditional Bulgarian salad as recommended by Benji, which is very similar to the Greek version without the cheese. It has taken us an hour and a half to get through the starter course as it seems after every mouthful Benji and Slobodan have to light and smoke a cigarette at the table.

Hooray, our main courses are here.

Oh dear. I ordered chicken and that is exactly what I have got-a chicken drumstick in the middle of a dinner plate. I have a cauldron of emotions and thoughts whizzing around my brain whilst I am staring transfixed at my plate. From 'where is the rest of it' to 'how the hell do I eat this in a ladylike manner' to 'I think I might explode with a fit of the giggles in a minute'.

I do not think laughing is what Mr Kurti has in mind. He is staring with disgust at his plate of a full fish, including the tail and eye, languishing in the middle of his empty plate staring at him.

"Three hours for a fish!" he has seethed, through his interpreter Albana, of course.

Third Day

All the delegates have left now and I am on the way to the airport with a very disconcerted Len. It appears that when we returned to the hotel last night, he decided to have a nightcap in the bar. As he approached the counter, the barman asked, "Yes, sir, what can I get you?"

"I will have a double brandy," came the reply.

"Is there anything else, sir?" The barman enquired.

"No, thank you," Len responded.

"Would you like a woman, sir?" The barman queried pointing to the group of 'ladies of the night' sat in the corner.

"Oh no, thank you," a polite but uncomfortable Len replied.

"You like a man then, sir?" The knowing barman asked.

"No, thank you," replied a startled Len.

"Oh," responded Mr Helpful, "would you like both?"

Len looked at him with what I can only reflect as an offended stance and uttered words I never actually knew anyone said, "Oh no, I couldn't possibly, I'm English."

Project Presentation to EU in Brussels.

Colin has presented the system to the EU in The Hague; it was deemed as a success.

BA (Hons) Business Studies Degree Final Year

Yay! I have passed the five-year course with a 2:1.

Who would have thought a girl from Oldham, eh?

Executive Summary
BA(Hons) Business Studies Degree
Sheffield Business School
Sheffield Hallam University 1999
INVESTIGATION INTO LIW AND THE IMPACT ON THE ORGANISATION AND IT'S PEOPLE
Vivienne Garland

Introduction

In 1992, Royal Mail underwent a change which was the most radical in its 360-year history; it restructured on a massive scale within one year. In 1994, RM Consulting was formed, Royal Mail's Internal Consultancy Services group, serving the Post Office in the UK and many overseas postal administrations directly or through BPCS. When RM Consulting was formed, there were over 1000 consultants drawn from a variety of backgrounds, located on three main sites in the UK at London, Swindon and Chesterfield.

In January 1999, RM Consulting moved into the Post Offices Services Group as part of the Shaping for Competitive Success (SCS) programme. The aim of SCS is to develop the whole Post Office Organisation to give a much clearer focus on customers' needs and market developments. Its aim is to make the organisation more flexible, quicker at decision making and therefore much more competitive across a range of markets. The move of RM Consulting as part of this programme was the first step to try and strengthen the market focus and provide Post Office customers with sharper specifications for the delivery areas of the business. This strategic change meant that RM Consulting had the status of a post office supplier rather than solely a Royal Mail supplier.

At the end of April 1999, Post Office Consulting was formed joining RM Consulting and Post Office Counter's Business Consultancy and Information Systems Consultancy. The move made Post Office Consulting one of the largest consultancies in the country and is intended to be the enabler for it to offer its knowledge products Post Office-wide in support of the corporation's commercial strategy and the businesses being set up as part of Shaping for Competitive Success proposals.

The commercial philosophy that accompanies Post Office Consulting demands flexibility, responsiveness and a constant drive to provide value for money for the Post Office's customers. One of the major initiatives aimed at meeting these objectives was the Location Independent Working Programme, LIW which began in 1993, when the consultancy was known as RM Consultancy.

My Article Published in Effective Consulting 2000

In this article, Viv Cockram considers aspects of Location Independent Working (LIW), through a case study on 'Consignia'—the new name for The Post Office Group, which includes Royal Mail, Parcelforce Worldwide and Post Office branches. When you were a child, did you ever have one of those India rubber power balls?

You threw it at the wall with the intention of catching it on the first bounce, but, in reality, it hit the wall, shot behind your head, skimmed the window, next door's shed, the dustbin lid, hit the wall and back into your hand, while you performed manoeuvres worthy of a contortionist. Learning is a lot like that. I commenced studying two GCSEs while working part-time and raising three children and ended (for the moment) with a dissertation on Location Independent Working (LIW) while pursuing a full-time career with Consignia and still caring for three children.

What is LIW?

LIW is not simply 'working from home', rather it enables work to be performed from a variety of locations with the functionality normally available within the base office environment. The convergence of computing and communications technologies has the effect of broadening the channels available for organisations, and this convergence has meant that, instead of people having to organise their work around a central office, they can ask the question: "What is the best place and time to suit the task in hand?"

LIW was introduced fully in Consignia in 1997 after piloting the concept. From this pilot, certain benefits and drawbacks were identified (see below). The research I undertook was to determine if these benefits and drawbacks had been realised and if the programme was successful. More importantly, it was also to discover whether LIW is truly a tool to achieve flexibility and what, if any, were the underlying issues involved?

Why did I choose LIW as a research topic?

In 1993, Consultancy Services Group of Consignia was asking itself, "Is LIW an initiative to meet the commercial philosophy, demanding flexibility, responsiveness and a constant drive to provide value for money for Consignia customers?" On a personal level, I chose LIW as my topic for research because I wanted to investigate an area which had change management and cultural issues at its core.

LIW has now been recognised by Consignia as an accepted workstyle and the main findings I identified during a six-month pilot study, which led to the LIW implementation, were as follows:

- *Drawbacks*
- *Some feelings of isolation*
- *Fear of loss of identity*
- *Reduced social interaction*
- *Danger of extended hours*
- *Problems with remote access to the technical network*
- *Benefits*
- *More time with clients*
- *Reduction in time to complete tasks*
- *Improved communication*
- *Less travel and stress*
- *More time to plan and organise*
- *Reduced accommodation costs (25%)*

It has been eight years now from the programme's infancy and I wanted to determine if these findings were still relevant now LIW has 'come of age'.

Old work routines are the last bastion of the old culture; any change within an organisation alters the cultural context; old rituals need to be abandoned and new ones created. Consignia's roots lie in a very hierarchical and public sector mindset which is no longer applicable in the rapidly changing business environment. The old structures and work practices act as a barrier to knowledge management and more flexible working. The introduction of LIW had the original aims of introducing flexible working and contributing to the overall achievement of the organisation. The original LIW project brief stated that LIW had to be:

- *Forward looking, responsive, creative and imaginative in the use of accommodation.*
- *Efficient and effective in the use of resources to provide the best possible value for money.*
- *Supportive of developing flexible and highly motivated people in teams with the skills necessary for business success.*

The concept of LIW, by definition, covers a wide area, the word 'independent', linked with 'location' proclaiming a geographical, and possibly psychological, variance from the centralised organisation. My research was performed over a six-month period, the findings being obtained primarily via questionnaire and through one-to-one interviews, both with people within the programme and with those operating within a 'normal' working environment. It should be noted the results obtained are indicative rather than absolute due to the following:

- *The percentage of responses was less than 100% (actual = 60%).*
- *The difficulty in quantifying some of the issues.*

- *The answers were mainly personal perceptions rather than truly imperative responses.*

The main observation I made while collating the results was regarding the amount of replies received and the speed with which they were returned. It is quite clear that, with a majority of the respondents, a great deal of time, effort and consideration had gone into answering the questions, and not a little humour. The overriding impression though was that the subject was something that the respondents were passionately committed to and that they felt deeply about some of the issues surrounding it. Flexibility achieved?

The research performed would indicate that LIW does work as a change management tool and supports its original aim of making Consignia a more flexible and responsive organisation. There were many questions within the research relating to the area of flexibility. One question in particular produced interesting responses around this area; this concerned the contact with clients and whether all participants working LIW within the research were asked, "How would you react if the programme was withdrawn?" The response was very clear and adamant in favour of its continuation, with 84% of the respondents using vocabulary such as 'dismay', 'disappointment' and 'unhappiness' at the thought of it being withdrawn. Many of the replies expressed were of the same theme, although not as eloquent as this response, "I believe it is the key enabler which supports a knowledge business and withdrawing it would be a major psychological factor affecting my motivation and loyalty to the business. I enjoy working for man organisation which takes my needs seriously; withdrawing LIW would affect my view of this. In addition, I think it would send out completely demoralising messages to people in the organisation about the innovativeness and effectiveness of Consignia."

Management Approach

Whilst achieving flexibility through a network approach requires a consistent technical infrastructure, a consistent management approach to LIW is also essential. LIW, like any new work routine, needs effective communication to reinforce role models and the language of change—and the management approach to it needs to be consistent across the organisation.

There are strong preconceptions surrounding LIW and these can lead to managers involuntarily (or otherwise) building obstacles to change. This may be particularly true of an organisation such as Consignia which has a highly homogenous culture. It is therefore imperative that the high performing managers should visibly support the change effort involved with LIW, and their efforts should in turn be supported by senior managers' behaviour throughout all Consignia. My research shows that there is not a consistent approach to the subject of LIW. This is especially true amongst non-LIW personnel, where the programme is seen as allowing some people to work away from the 'norm' and therefore allowed to be less productive—in other words, LIW is viewed as a 'skivers' charter'.

Cultural intent

Early in 1999, Peter Boalch, Consulting Partner, presented a draft statement of cultural intent for Consignia.

He described the 'spirit' and 'ethos' of the organisation being joined together with its Purpose, Direction and Values to form the cultural intent. From this, it is clear that significant cultural change is taking place within our organisation and LIW is simply evidence of that change. Peter also went on to describe the future spirit of Consignia thus; "It's a democracy of diverse talents where belonging to a community of knowledge workers supports politics-free collaboration and a risk-taking-but-blame-free climate."

Consignia is recognised as a commercially successful, leading edge knowledge business, but it's only for the brave—there are no functional foxholes to hide in—and for those who like work to be both fulfilling and exciting. In fact, it's a fun place to be. "It is my belief that LIW. supports this vision by providing Consignia with the means to be in the right place at the right time so that it can capture, use and share the knowledge and skills it has with whomever it needs to. LIW allows people to more easily assess situations 'on site' and empowers them to make informed decisions—be they risky or not."

Consignia is trying to move away from 'turfism'. However, my research produced evidence that it may have a long way to go. But there are encouraging signs that Consignia is at least on the road to eliminating the old, stagnant culture. Many people stated a belief that LIW is a key enabler which supports a knowledge business and that Consignia is following enlightened policies of investment in employees.

Viv Cockram

Following a varied career as a Shop Assistant, Credit Controller and Assistant Buyer in a large department store, Viv joined Consignia in 1993. Starting as a helpline operator at Consignia's information Technology Service, she moved to technical support for the Royal Mail Generic Track and Trace project and then joined Consignia's consulting service in 1996, initially as an Application Manager before moving to the Business Systems working on various Consignia projects as a Business Analyst. Viv has recently completed a five-year part-time BA Honours Business Studies degree.

My Second Article Published in Effective Consulting 2001

Viv Cockram visited Bulgaria when she was working for British Postal Consultancy Service (BPCS), the international consultancy arm of former Consignia Plc, on a European Union funded PHARE (Poland and Hungary Assistance for the Recovery of the Economy) project.

The PHARE programme was established by the EU to assist Central and Eastern European countries in economic reform—mainly of infrastructure industries. She was involved in a project on developing key account management for postal operators in six countries and her objective was to develop a database in Microsoft Access that would assist key account managers in their everyday work. As a result of the project, Bulgaria Post now have a dedicated key account management team managing the needs of their largest clients. BPCS provide postal consultancy throughout the world in all aspects of postal business and have a reputation for the quality of their work and their in-depth knowledge of their sector.

Do My Eyes Deceive Me?

There are times in your life when you just cannot trust your eyes to see the truth. Anyone who has met a prospective life partner in a darkened, noisy disco, only to discover later that you made a date with an alien from the planet 'Zorg', will understand. This type of inadequacy seemed to afflict me the first time I worked in Sofia, Bulgaria. The challenge to my rational thought and failing eyesight happened when, ascending a set of subway stairs in the centre of Sofia, I came eye to eye with two live guinea pigs, with a piece of carrot and lettuce for company, sitting on a fishing stool.

At first, I could not believe what I was seeing, but upon realising that it was what I thought it was, I had to ask myself: "Why don't they run away?" After all, this was the capital city of Bulgaria where there was frantic movement all around, people rushing to and fro, cars driving by tooting horns and revving engines—but still the little furry rascals just sat there! The most peculiar thing was that there were no bars around them, no cage to hold them, yet they simply sat instead of scampering off.

The guinea pigs were for sale; their owner was one of Sofia's many unemployed trying to earn a living, which really meant that he was begging. His strong pride, however, would not allow him to beg outright, so here he was offering something in return for any small token of charity. This same principle was adopted by the shoelace sellers and the many men, women and children (some as young as four) who were covered in bruises and squatting on the floor beside a pair of battered weigh-scales. Now, I know that every capital city has its so called 'underclass', but Sofia's beggars seemed to come from a greater stratum of the overall population. Why? The answer probably lies in Bulgaria's geographical position and its current demography.

Blood Money

Recently, I read an article by Mileana Dimova which described a harrowing new trade now common in Bulgaria; the commodity however, is not guinea pigs or even shoelaces but something far more basic—human blood.

The practice, which has existed over the past seven or eight years, is to 'advise' relatives of patients who will undergo an operation to donate certain quantities of blood, the blood type is irrelevant. The state hospitals have given the people of Bulgaria an ultimatum, provide blood or worry about the lives of their relatives. Unfortunately, not everybody can give blood, so they buy it. It could be viewed as a very sensible idea to buy blood if people are willing to sell it, since there is a great shortage, but as is common in Bulgaria, the practice is corrupt. Every morning in the centre of Sofia, a group of men gather outside the hospital with a view to making money. Their job, however, is simply to sell their blood and haggle over the price (Milena, DIMOVA, 1999). Thankfully, wherever I went in Sofia, I saw evidence of the unemployment but no personal evidence of this new bloody trade.

There are two parts of Milena's article with which I did identify, such as the description of the people who were selling their blood and the pervasive corruption. Milena described the men selling blood firstly as 'dark'. then later in her article as 'swarthy' and finally as 'Gypsies'. Her contempt at the actual practice of selling blood seemed to be somehow linked to the ethnicity of the people who were selling it. I do not wish to make a political comment, only to say that this 'perception' of the Gypsies was also evident as I walked around Sofia with my ethnic Bulgarian colleague. When approached by one beggar, a one-armed Gypsy woman, my Bulgaria colleague dismissed her contemptuously with: "Just ignore her, they have better houses than we do." This reaction perplexed me greatly, considering that minorities have been persecuted throughout history and I realised that any changes within Bulgaria would have to be targeted at a heart and mind level, and although I did not share the commonly held views of my Bulgarian friends with regard to the Gypsies, I did see ample evidence of the endemic corruption.

The Family Comes to Bulgaria

When working and travelling abroad, meanings do get altered in translation—there is no doubt of that—but some things are the same the world over. For one of my visits to Bulgaria, I stayed in a hotel which had thirty rooms on six floors and was elegantly decorated—in drastic contrast to the apartment blocks around it on the Maria Louisa Boulevard. Strangely, while I was there, I only ever saw one other guest. I did however, see plenty of other people. I saw the 'ladies of the night', lots of suited men sitting outside hotel rooms and one gentleman dripping in gold who, although not a guest, dined every night with the full attention of all the staff in the restaurant and hotel.

In my naivety, none of these facts made any connection in my mind. Even when I had seen the same gilded gentlemen enter other hotels, accompanied by the same flurry of attentiveness, I never dreamed that there was some nefarious activity taking place. It was not until the other 'real' guest in the hotel, a retired British policeman acting as a consultant to the Bulgarian State Police, asked me how I thought such a fine hotel functioned with only three of the thirty rooms occupied, that I suddenly understood what was occurring. I suppose up until that point, the gentleman in question would have had to look like Marlon Brando for me to register what was going on. It suddenly dawned on me that, while I had been in Sofia, I had never seen a single Bulgarian policeman. My fellow hotel guest explained that this was because the Bulgarian policeman was allocated a mere $35 per month for petrol and only ever 'ventured out into the city when a major crime occurred'. My fellow hotel guest had many interesting pieces of local crime-related gossip, including the startling story of the old lady who lived in a flat overlooking the national football stadium in Sofia. One fine evening, she was out on her balcony enjoying the air when the national team scored a goal. The football fans celebrated in their normal style of releasing rounds of automatic gunfire up into the air, and needless to say, one of the shots hit her! My retired policeman had many stories to tell me, including the one about the illegal production of branded whisky; unfortunately, I cannot give any more detail other than to say the colour is achieved through a very novel process!

So, what is the Bulgarian Government doing about it? In a speech in June 2001 to the government, the then Prime

Minister Ivan Kostov presented the measures the government would introduce to counteract crime and enforce law and order (BBC Worldwide Monitoring). These measures are probably as unstable as the country itself; how could they be anything else? In Bulgaria in 1946, the former monarch was exiled by the communists after the monarchy was abolished, a totalitarian police state followed and now, in an historic first for Eastern Europe, the same former monarch, King Simeon Saxe-Coburg-Gotha, accepted the vacant role of Prime Minister on 12 July 2001. So, full circle, it is no wonder the people of Bulgaria, never mind the police or the government, have no faith in the measures and reforms which are proposed.

Cultural Change

I found Bulgaria fascinating, the people friendly and approachable and most striking was that they always took the time to speak and show interest in whatever I was doing. Like many places, Bulgaria is full of contradictions: the crumbling offices with the most recent technology, the sumptuous hotels next to the run-down apartment blocks, the expensive sports cars driving on roads with no tarmac. I have always been fascinated in how culture affects the way people think and act, and in this instance, how the indicative culture of Bulgaria will affect the change process proposed. I do not pretend to understand all the cultural and political factors that are, and have been, affecting Bulgaria and the Balkans as they are so complex; indeed, if I did, I would probably be working for the UN. However, I would love to return to such a diverse country that made me so welcome to find out more, even though a further visit would probably leave me more confused!

I Did Not Learn This at School

Always be yourself because the people that matter don't mind and the ones that mind don't matter.

Royal Mail Consulting 2001

Oh no, it is him again.

I have managed to be promoted another two grades since starting in Royal Mail Consulting but I have hit the glass ceiling, if I am successful at this interview board, I am waiting to go into I will smash through and become a Senior Business Analyst in an extremely male-dominated industry.

I have hit a couple of barriers before I have even entered the room. Firstly, I have found out that one of the board is Tommy Shanklin again, and I know how he loves to play bad cop. Then Mr 'oh I just need to tell you this just as you are entering the door' has just informed me that there is an extra man on the board and he does not want me to get the promotion but one of his own team. What is the matter with this man? Why does he keep doing this? I know he is trying to wrong foot me but has he not learned anything from the last time? The young man from Human Resources is very apologetic and embarrassed because it is just not cricket.

Here we go then.

Oh god, there he is waiting to pounce. Things have gone fine, even the man who does not want me (allegedly) has not been aggressive or rude and more importantly, I have been able to answer his many questions.

Oh, here he comes with his antics, "What kind of leader are you?" No preamble, no hellos, he is just straight in there.

I have answered it satisfactorily I feel but he has taken exception to a comment I made about setting clear and achievable objectives.

"So, are you telling me that when you wake up in the morning, the first thing you think is oh, I will set clear and achievable objectives," he asked with what I have to say is a sneer, not an attractive look.

"Of course, not," I smiled sweetly, "but sometimes the situation demands clarification and focus," he will be telling me I am a clever little devil again in a minute.

"What?" He bellowed, very hostilely I have to say, "You come in work and think that do you?" He is pronouncing every word precisely; he sounds like my dad now.

"As I said," I responded calmly, "it depends on the situation and as a leader, you need to know your staff and their behaviours and more importantly, their limitations."

"Oh yea, you've got to know your staff's limitations, have you?" He sneered again; he is quite cross with me now.

"Yes, of course, you have to," I answered him looking straight in his eye.

"Come on then," he practically spat at me, "in your wisdom," he continued, he is essentially glaring at me now, "give us an example!"

"Well," I said slowly and calmly, "if I was a member of your staff and you told me to stand in that corner and hop up and down on my right leg for five minutes, you as my leader would know that that was an unachievable objective."

"Why?" He asked; he is getting really cross now.

"Because I have one leg shorter than the other and I would fall over."

Chesterfield College January 2004

I really do not know if I am up for this. What is wrong with me? You would have thought I would have learnt when I was at university.

No.

My absolutely humiliating, red faced, sweaty occasional appearances in front of class are now to be replaced by frequent events and to be a part of my everyday life. Never before at any point have I thought, *'Oh I want to teach.'* Never. My original one O Level is not the perfect indicator for a career in academia and even after my subsequent qualifications, a teaching career never even entered into my head for a minute. However, here I am embarking on a career as a Lecturer in A level equivalent Business Studies at a College of Further Education.

It is being a blended family that started it all.

I did not think, well we are a merged unit, so now I will teach; it is not as random as that but it was the introduction of two boy siblings into an all-girl family that did it. I had no idea that parenting male offspring would be so markedly different than raising a female brood. To be honest, it was not so much the eldest son James that was my downfall but the younger one Graham.

It is all my fault to be truthful, although some would argue that there were other forces at work, including Graham. The bottom line is that I should have dealt with things differently; I should have treated him the same as my biological children, but I did not. I let him get away with things that they never would have been allowed to.

My attitude was altered right from the start but was cemented with the bedroom situation, not with the allocation of the rooms but my attitude in cleaning those sleeping quarters. Having teenagers of any sex is a whole new parenting ballgame and I quickly came to realise that one of the mechanisms I would need to introduce, if only for my own sanity, was not to clean or tidy their bedrooms. The only thing I did do was go in and strip the bed, wash the bedding and remake the bed afterwards.

Problem number one—I felt that I could not even enter into the boy's domains. I did not want to go into any of the kid's rooms or 'pits' to be perfectly honest but it was as though there was an invisible force stopping me going in James' or Graham's rooms. The introduction of two male teenagers into the household when I had never had them from babies and growing up took some getting used to, not their fault, mine entirely. I felt like I was invading their privacy, that I had no right to go in, that I was some kind of interloper, bottom line, that I was not their mum. It was agreed by all parties concerned that I would ask for the bedding, they would strip the bed, I would wash and dry the covers and then they would remake with the clean bed linen.

Excellent.

Problem number two—this worked for James and the girls but was a different kettle of fish with Graham.

Every week, I asked for the flaming things, several times during the seven-day period and every week not a stitch was forthcoming. It reached a point where I had to have a word with myself, if it had been the girls I would have said, "Get in there and strip that bloody bed now!" But no. I did not chastise him, moan at him, question him, direct him, I just let him do whatever he wanted.

It got to the situation after the umpteen thwarted request where I thought to myself, *'Get in there yourself and get the chuffing things, it's your bloody house.'*

Oh, my god.

It was challenging to get the bed linen to say the least and oh my word, there was a handkerchief in that bed that looks more like a piece of origami! Mr C is going to have to have a word with him.

"You are going to have to talk to him, it's not nice going in there and finding what I did," I exclaimed.

"No," was the response from Mr C.

"I know I have never had boys and so was a bit blindsided, it's not just because it's a bit gross…" I trailed off, after trying to explain.

"No," was the constant reply.

"Yes," I continued, "and also, you know if he is doing anything with his girlfriend in there, it's illegal, they are only fourteen."

"Mmm, yes," change of tack now from Mr C.

"I am not naïve, you know, I know teenagers do it, but that girl is under our roof and it's our responsibility," I chuntered on.

"Mmm, yes," came the mumble.

"Yes, and I know that boys do things, even though I have no experience of it with the girls."

"Mmm, yes," was the predictable response.

"It's not very nice for me, you know," I said wailing slightly.

"No," was the answer

"Can't he just do it in the bathroom?" I questioned mildly hysterically.

"Erm," Mr Eloquent replied.

"You are just going to have to have a word with him," I responded as I flounced out of the dining room.

Mr C's talk did not go as planned. Graham now thinks he has an illegal handkerchief.

What has any of this got to do with me teaching?

Well, Graham has been with us for three years now, has left school at sixteen and wants to do a Computer Studies course at Chesterfield College. The fact that this has a three-day itinerary and his current girlfriend is on a three-day hairdressing course at the same college is just a coincidence apparently. I do not think he has fully thought it through as it could be that both courses are not run on exactly the same days.

I asked him if he wanted me to go to the interview with him, and he does, so I have arranged to meet him outside the co-op at a quarter to five to give us enough time to get to college, find the room etc. for the five-thirty interview as neither of us have been before.

Where the hell is he?

It is now five o'clock and the bus from our home has just arrived and he has not alighted, there is not another one for twenty minutes.

Perhaps, he is coming a different way?

Erm, I do not think so as it is now ten minutes past five. A text to Mr C has elicited the response that he thinks I should just leave him to it and I should go home, but I am not, it is important, even though Graham obviously does not think so.

The later bus has just arrived, and low and behold there he is, wearing a woolly hat as protection against the rain, I on the other hand, am absolutely soaking wet through.

And then it happened. The three years of not telling him off, of letting him get away with practically everything, of me just not being me, the seal was broken and oooo, there I am.

I was being very calm but direct up until the point I asked him the question as we traversed the doughnut roundabout, "Do you think I am cross?"

"Yes," came the sheepish reply.

"I am not cross; I am fucking furious."

I am like a fishwife, my swearing and screaming would make a soldier blush. I have continued in this manner until we have approached the college and I have settled into a seething silence after I have located the room and have both taken a seat with all the other prospective college goers.

Something strange has happened; he is still wearing his woolly hat. Graham is nothing if not polite and has been brought up to remove any headgear when indoors, but that bobble hat remains firmly on his head. Just as I was going to ask what was occurring, a lady lecturer has come in and said, "Can all Office Administration Students follow me upstairs, the Computer Studies students remain here, you will all be called alphabetically for your interviews." Every single girl in the room has got up out of their seats and followed the lady, whilst all the boys have remained where they are to await their interview by one of the three male lecturers siting behind the three desks.

Oh, we are being called immediately as our surname starts with C. We have still not spoken to each other since we have arrived and he has still got that flipping hat on. As we sat down, two things occurred simultaneously, the lecturer introduced himself as 'Nev' and Graham took his hat off.

It was as if time stood still, and what happened next seemed like forever but was probably only a nanosecond. I wish someone had taken a photograph of my face because I can imagine it would be highly amusing. I just stared at Graham open mouthed whilst examining the work that had been performed by his trainee hairdresser girlfriend that afternoon; he was completely bald. Graham had not taken his hat off as his manners would normally dictate because it was obvious that he thought I would go off absolutely alarming when presented with the vision of his hairless head seeing as how I had acted like a fishwife just because he was late.

Well, I have lost it. I am crying with laughter and I am apologising to Nev because I am laughing so much, I am snorting slightly and I am having trouble with reoccurring giggles throughout this whole interview. Nev has offered Graham a place on the course which is good and before we leave, I just have to ask Nev an associated question, "How come all the girls in the room went upstairs for Office Administration and it is only boys on the Computer Studies course?"

"It is like this every year," he responded, "there are never any girls wanting to do it."

"Why not?" I enquired. "I work in IT and I am female."

"Do you want to come and teach with us?" Came the response.

So, that is where it started and here is where it has finished. The Royal Mail IT Consulting Department was bought by the Prism Alliance along with the rest of IT and as part of the deal, a substantial amount of money was put aside for voluntary redundancy. I have had a miraculous career in Royal Mail, even smashing through the glass ceiling, rising eight grades in eleven years but the culture in the Alliance is completely different. It is focused totally on cost rather than people and so ironically, I decided to take the money.

I returned to Chesterfield College and spoke to Nev and he thought I would be better suited to teaching in the Business Department and so did Sue, the department head and so, here I am, ready to teach my first lesson in Advanced Vocational Certificate of Education (AVCE) Marketing and Promotional Strategy.

Oh my god, I am nervous.

I have been working up to this moment for weeks; I have had to acquire a whole new set of skills just to get to this point to produce a scheme of work, lesson plans, resources etc. I was given a curriculum paper on the subject and basically told to get on with it.

They are all staring at me.

"Okay, let's go round the room, one by one, tell me your name and something about yourself." I am hoping by linking a piece of personal information to a person will let me remember their names.

Well, I will definitely remember his name, he has just called me a 'bitch' under his breath.

Chesterfield College November 2004

Give me strength, I must be bonkers.

The Colander Boys, I ask you.

I have been given another cohort of AVCE students; I must have done something right last time. My boss Colin made a throw away comment, "Why don't you get them to market and promote something real?" I thought about it and came up with an idea, we have a café run by students in the department as Catering is an area within Business and said café is open to the public. The coffee bar/restaurant has just had a rebrand and is now called @SPIRE2—play on words and all that, so it seemed the ideal opportunity to use that as the inspiration.

What have I let myself in for?

I got them to divide into groups, which funnily enough completely mirror the class seating arrangements, so that made five teams in total and tasked them to come up with a concept. Once all five concepts had been presented, they would then vote for the one they liked the best and then the whole class would help the winning team 'hone' the theory ready for implementation.

That went really well, they all enjoyed it and got really invested and one team was the clear runaway concept winning in the voting round.

Good grief.

The concept of the winning team is to emulate the Calendar Girls film, this depicts a group of Women's Institute ladies getting naked, hiding their rude bits behind cakes and buns and such. The victorious team is a group of six boys and we have had some extremely animated debate within the class, the idea is for them to hide their bodies behind specific pieces of equipment related to baking. The deliberation around what the group should be called arrived at the selection of the name 'The Colander Boys' with the 'Naked Chef' coming a close second in the class voting.

Next is to decide how to move forward, but this has left me with a bit of a quandary which I have discussed with Colin.

"I know that most of them are nearly eighteen, but I can't let them all be naked, can I?"

"No, there are issues around nakedness, you are right," Colin concurred.

"Yes, I think one of them is only just seventeen too, plus I think some people higher up might have something to say if I let them be starkers except for a kitchen utensil," I stated.

"Yes, I think you need to tone it down," he agreed.

I laughed out loud and replied, "I know but you know what they are like, they are like yea we want be naked, no clothes nothing,"

"You can't let that happen," he confirmed.

"No, I will have to come up with a compromise that keeps dignity intact, keeps their parents and college management off my back but allows them their desire to show their bodies off!"

The concession we have agreed to, which I put to the whole class, is that they will be fully clothed waist down but they will remove their shirts and wear an unbuttoned waistcoat to flash a bit of flesh. Everyone was happy with this, although Jonathan says he is a bit shy and Adam has dropped out because 'his girlfriend wouldn't like him to show his flesh off'.

Dear me, this was not something I thought I would be discussing when I started to teach.

What to do next?

I have been to our Advertising Department and arranged a photoshoot with the five remaining boys in the café. I have organised the procurement of the waistcoats which they are now wearing shirtless, with varying degrees of embarrassment, excitement and showing off emanating from the boys. I have let them pick their own utensil to pose with and George from advertising has taken a variety of shots in the café, group, duets, and even one with me in the middle of them all.

We have now come out into the college onto the main spiral staircase as it is fully glazed and George thinks this will provide great light for the photos. I have just spent the last thirty minutes running up and down the flipping staircase, making sure no unsuspected students come upon our models. This is not a concern for the other students but a direct request from our shyer participants. I do not know how they are going to cope when these photos are published and more to the point, I am absolutely shattered from running up and down and shepherding people in the opposite direction.

George has just rung me and asked me to go up and look at the photos, he feels there may be an issue with some of them taken in the café.

I have laughed out loud, startling a couple of people in the open office in the process, the little buggers. My mistake was to let them choose their own 'utensils' themselves and I was so caught up in making sure they were smiling, pouting, looking moody or whatever facial expressions they were displaying that I had not noticed what they were doing with said implements. Needless to say, we have had to use airbrushing software to remove several instances of a strategically placed erect rolling pin.

George has sent the photos out to his contacts at the free newspaper establishments in the area and most of them have run with the story and published them, including in one edition a photo with me in which I was not expecting. It has caused a lot of excitement in the classroom, not least because the BBC at Derby have got hold of the story and are featuring it on their internet site.

Chesterfield College 2005

Something has got to give.

As well has the AVCE teaching, I have been allocated other classes which include, General Certificate of Secondary Education (GCSE) Business Studies and Study Skills for sixteen-to-eighteen-year olds and Institute of Leadership and Management Level 3 for Adults. I am studying for my teaching qualification and now, how I do not know, I am writing bids for funding for courses and such for the college. There is no way to sustain this level of activity.

I have decided that at the end of the academic year, I will stop teaching the younger people and concentrate on the adults. This seems to be a sensible approach as the AVCE qualification is being reviewed and the other two daytime subjects have caused me some issues.

The study skills are first thing on a Monday morning and although there is not too much teaching involved there is an awful lot of 'corralling' to do. As the lesson is held in a computer room, all the students want to do is catch up with their friends via email to find out what they have been up to during the weekend. This does not tax me too much as there is a central switch which I can utilise if I feel they are spending too much time chatting or whatever online. The main problem is that the room is on the 7th floor and there is absolutely no chance of getting in a lift at that time of day and so consequently, I spend the first fifteen minutes of the lesson unable to speak or get my breath.

The GCSE Business Studies has nearly been my undoing and almost caused me to give up teaching altogether. There is a strange culture in college which is so much different to Royal Mail. For example, I had no idea there was a Christmas meal out for the department, when I queried why it was not advertised the answer was that they did not want anybody to feel bad about saying that they did not want to go. How you were supposed to find out about the event in the first place? I have no idea. Whereas in IT, every Thursday night was drinks night around town and there were numerous company sessions throughout the year which were highly promoted.

This culture then filtered into the classroom and it was the Graham situation all over again. I did not know how to behave or deal with the different situations presented. The class was on a Friday afternoon, so that was a pain to start with; the students had to attend in most cases just that afternoon on that day, so motivation was not high. Secondly, I had to teach it in a computer room where there was no central switch and so could not control what they were doing online. Thirdly, most of them were on it to get paid thirty pounds a week through a government scheme and so attention or an interest in the subject was not necessarily there.

The first week I did my usual; get them to stand up, tell me their name and then something interesting about themselves. This worked on the whole until latecomer Mark turned up ten minutes after the lesson started. I should have marked him as late which could result in him not getting his money that week, but I would never do that; I could not bring myself to enact that part of the culture. It was alien to me, taking the register was bad enough, putting a late indicator was just not going to happen, they are supposed to be here because they want to not because they were made to attend like at school.

"Oh hello," I said, "we have just been going around the class, introducing ourselves."

"Uh," replied grumpy.

"Can you stand up please and tell us your name and something interesting about yourself?" I asked.

"I'm not standing up," was the reply.

"Okay, well stay sat down then and introduce yourself," I responded.

"You introduce yourself," was the answer.

"Well, if you had been here on time, you would have heard it," I smiled sweetly, "but seeing as you weren't, I will repeat it just for you," which I did.

He just stared at me belligerently.

"What is your name?" I persisted.

"Mark," answered Mr Sulky.

"And can you tell us something interesting about yourself?" I questioned.

"No," was the reply.

I was not giving up. "What? There is nothing you can tell us about yourself?"

"No"

"You don't support Arsenal then? I thought you must do seeing as you are wearing an Arsenal football shirt?"

He looked at me with grudging respect although he did not answer and he has given me that respect ever since; it was obviously a test and I had passed.

However, although I succeeded in that one, there were other challenges to which I did not seem to be doing well at. From a very nice boy who would not get off his phone, to a boy who was always trying to hangout of the third-floor window to the young Asian guy who I suspected was some kind of dealer. I tried without success to deal with the issues whilst trying to follow the culture of the college and after six weeks was at my wits end.

"Colin, I cannot do this," I wailed, "I don't know what to do."

"Be yourself," came the answer.

So, a lot quicker than I did with Graham, I acted like me.

"Right!" This word works like a charm with my kids and pets. "You turn your phone off or I will treat you like a child and take it off you, you do not try to do any of your wheeling or dealing in my class and you get away from that window and sit down."

They all looked at me with a mixture of expressions on their faces to which I responded, "Oh, don't worry, I will not enforce these measures, I've already spoken to security and they will be up here as soon as I need them."

The last two have not returned to class and I have lost count of the times I have sent the phone mad boy out of class. It has gotten to the point that I do not even say anything; I just stand with the door open and out he goes.

I feel at the end of this course, even though I definitely do not want to teach it again, I have been successful and mainly because of Mark, Mr Grumpy. *'There are obviously academic targets associated with the course and the college are measured on them but there are other "learning activities" that take place that cannot be measured but are just as important,'* I think. Mark is an exceptionally clever and gifted person but has had some problems at home which resulted in him going to living with his aunt instead of him staying at home. As I have got to know him over the year, he has opened up to me and told me that he does nothing in the house to help his aunt and she pays for everything and has even bought him a car. Over time with the help of another student who lives at home and works every spare hour in his dad's shop for no wage or any other benefit I have manged to get 'through' to Mark that does he not feel that he should 'help' his aunt is someway. It turns out, he does, and although he did not pass the course, not because of ability, but because of his erratic attendance, he informed on his last lesson with me that he had got a job three evenings a week delivering pizza. Although he did not give his aunt any of his wages, he did not ask her for any spending money for his car etc. Result.

I take that as a win.

Chesterfield College 2006

Never in a million years did I think when I started to teach that I would be squaring up to a burly bouncer on a Friday night in downtown Chesterfield on behalf on Chesterfield College.

Why?

I have no idea, well I know why I am squaring up to him, because he is being aggressive towards Christine, but why I am out with her doing what we are doing I have no idea. These things just seem to happen. One minute, I am in college minding my own business, the next, it is arranged that I will go around all the venues in Chesterfield that have bouncers or door people with Christine to try and persuade them to take a college course.

Are they mad?

To work in the UK as a door supervisor (bouncer) or a security guard, you have to have a Security Industry Association (SIA) licence. The licence was created in 2001 along with the Security Industry Association to regulate the UK private security industry to improve the quality of service, raise standards and remove criminal elements and criminality.

The SIA created a course called the Level 2 Working as a Door Supervisor within the Private Security Industry (catchy title) to go along with the licence which you have to pass before you qualify for the licence.

The course includes four modules:

1. Working within the private security industry.

2. Working as a door supervisor in the security industry.

3. Conflict management within the private security industry.

4. Physical intervention with the private security industry.

Failure to secure a SIA licence whilst continuing to work on the doors could result in six months imprisonment or five thousand pound fine.

No pressure then.

The trouble is, none of the bouncers want to do the course, it has taken five years to even get it to be available at

Chesterfield College in the first place. Added to that issue is that traditionally the bouncers of Chesterfield are run by two feuding families, and even when doormen from Derby were brought in to diffuse the situation, it is still a bit of a cauldron. Enter into this arena, me and Christine, we did not stand a cat in hells chance of getting them to do the course. We have been around all the pubs, obviously having a drink in each one and although none of the bouncers were outwardly aggressive until the last drinking establishment, it is quite obvious that two women are not going to change the cultural behaviour of God knows how many years overnight even if one of the ladies did used to run one of the pubs. This prior comradeship was the main problem at the last hostelry, that and the fact that Christine was getting a trifle feisty with more bravado than required as the alcohol imbued rose. All hell broke loose and little old me has had to stand between her and a very belligerent burly doorman and it was at that point that I called it a day and ushered Christine off to a taxi and sent her on her way home.

To be perfectly honest, I have been involved in so many things in the name of college that I never thought I would ever be. From getting participants from local hotels, restaurants and the Chinese Association to take a one-day course of Wine Appreciation, resulting in a very drunken trio from a local hotel who decided that as the Chinese Association were only going to sniff the eighteen different bottles of wine provided that they would drink them all, to dealing with slightly squiffy mayoral representatives, to any event containing the word 'French' in the title to hosting a young French catering student for five weeks. It is Walsh's/House of Fraser all over again, I just seem to 'fall' into these situations which really have nothing to do with me, but end up with me participating or even taking charge. To be honest, it is Sue, she drags me into all sorts from Young Enterprise to writing a script for a college video and sourcing a professional company to shoot it to visiting the Houses of Parliament. Well, that was not so much her, but the College Principal.

The College Principal will tell anyone who wants to hear, and those who do not, that he does not know how I did it, but one day he just looked up from his desk and there I was sat looking at him. You need to understand his bafflement at this state of affairs is because his domain is only entered into after running the gauntlet of the two secretaries that are stationed outside his office with what seems to be the sole intention of stopping access to this realm. It is the whole college culture again, but to be honest, it is no challenge at all to me after dealing with the likes of Tommy Shanklin and his ilk and subsequently, I am in his office regularly discussing all sorts of things, much to the annoyance of the two secretaries and most of the directors.

On this occasion, I am as baffled as he is.

"You want me to go where?" I asked in total bemusement.

"The Houses of Parliament," came the response.

"The Houses of Parliament?" I replied in total confusion.

"Yes, and take some employers with you," he added.

"Why?" I responded still no wiser on any of it.

"Because that's what they want," he answered.

"Who?" I screeched slightly.

"Well, I don't want to go, do I?" He stated incredulously.

Well, that it is as clear as mud. I have noticed when you talk to people who are incredibly academic, they do not always speak the same language as us mere mortals.

"What?" It was all I could think to say, my mum would not be happy. I should have at least said 'pardon', very rude of me.

"You know all the employers, don't you?" He said exasperated.

What has that got to do with it and it is no good you getting shirty with me is what I thought but what I replied, was "What am I doing with them?"

The conversation went on for way too long in this manner until I finally managed to decipher the information presented and determine some kind of logic. It appears I need to take at least two employer representatives with me to The Houses of Commons to participate in some sort of University and College Employer Forum collaboration. And just to keep the top brass at college happy, I have to take the Marketing Director with me as well.

Oh.

I did get two employers and the Marketing Director to go with me and off to The Houses of Parliament we went; I was still none the wiser as to what we were supposed to be doing when we got there but the others did not seem bothered as it was a day away from work and a trip to London.

On arrival, we were met at visitor entrance number nine at the Palace of Westminster by our local Member of Parliament who was ours for the day to show us around. He did an admiral job even showing us where the Queen's private loo was behind a screen which she utilised if she needed to when she opened Parliament. We went in the Houses of Commons and listened to a debate about some trees near a railway line, had a look in the House of Lords and then went to meet the other representatives of the universities/colleges invited. What followed was a few speeches and lots of drinking of wine. As we made our way out, there were two things that happened.

We were walking through St Stephens Chapel and people were walking and passing in both directions when I saw a man I recognised, but I just could not place him. As he walked past, he looked at me and said, "Hello, love" in a very deep voice. It was not until later that the penny dropped and I realised it was John Prescott, he must have thought I was a right plonker. The second occurrence was that it turns out that our Member of Parliament's son is in fact in the same class at school as my youngest daughter. He knows her well because when she has domestic science; she tells us what she is making and invariably we say we do not want it, poor girl, so once she has made whatever dish we have declined, she gives it to the son who then takes it home to his family for them to eat.

Small world.

Eskilstuna, Sweden December 2007

I have always wanted my name shouted over an airport address system—not.

My role at college does not seem to be slowing down. I have stopped teaching the younger people but still teach adults, at college, on employer premises including the local hospital education centre and I still write bids for funding. One of the bids I have been successful with is a Centre of Vocational Excellence in Logistics and they asked me to run the COVE as well.

I do not even drive, but hey ho, that is not a barrier, I co-ordinated the design of three Engineering Degrees but I have never been an engineer, either. As part of my COVE role, I went to talk to the Transport Organisation about a Hiab (Hydrauliska Industria HB which is an acronym for the Finnish company invented it) simulator they were trialling.

A Hiab driver is someone who loads, transports and offloads goods from a vehicle that has a lorry-mounted crane attached. If your work is going to involve loading and offloading goods from a vehicle that has a lorry-mounted crane attached, you will need a HIAB training licence; also sometimes referred to as an ALLMI Certificate.

Qualification as a HIAB driver can be gained through various training companies. Successful completion of this would entail completing an assessment to prove your competence. There is also an opportunity to undertake a practical test at a later date for those who find it difficult to complete the assessment.

In order to complete the course, you would need to be 18 years of age or older and have a valid Certificate of Professional Competence (CPC). You would also require full health and eyesight clearance, an enhanced DBS disclosure certificate, a European Standard CESE Safety Certificate and hold a full UK Driving Licence.

The problem is that they want to get young people into the industry but there are so many hoops they need to jump through before they can even start the course; they do not have the ability, opportunity or legal requirements to practice on a HIAB in the first place. Enter the simulator which was designed by a Swedish Research Company in Stockholm to prove that you could not train on a simulator. It turns out that they proved the complete opposite and now have a commercial market success on their hands. After seeing it with the transport people, I am off to Sweden to buy one for the college.

Of course, I am not allowed to go on my own, even though the project I manage is funding the trip, we have co-ordinated it with the Catering Department and a school we have a relationship with in Eskistuna. Therefore, two lecturers from that department are going, Jim and Linda and the College Principal has decided to come along. The two lecturers will spend all the time at the corresponding college in Sweden, whereas the Principal and myself will spend the first day with the research team in Stockholm, and the following morning at the college, and then we will all return back to the UK.

I have had to arrange everything, from transport, to hotels to flights and Jim, Linda and myself are waiting in a mini-bus in a carpark off the M1 near Derby awaiting the arrival of the Principal.

Oh my god, what has he come as?

He is wearing a full-length leather coat and a leather Stetson; he looks like a cross between a cattle rancher and a trawlerman.

All has gone well, we got to Heathrow and through the airport and onto the flight to Stockholm without any incidents. The Principal has come in very handy as he used to work in Sweden for three years and therefore speaks Swedish and so has purchased the required train tickets to Eskilstuna on our behalf. Jim and Linda are absolutely terrified of him, will not sit next to him and leave any conversation, questions or comments in my hands; I do not know what they think he will do to them.

The first evening has gone well, we have met the teachers from the Swedish college in an 'English Pub' in downtown Eskistuna. It is really a square shop unit, with a bar and a lot of brasses and old plates displayed on the wall, and oh my god, the drinks are extortionately expensive. We have all returned to the hotel for a good night's sleep which I think may elude me as I have a walk-in wardrobe in my chamber which is at least ten degrees colder than the rest of the room and there is definitely something in there other than shelves and clothes.

The visit to Stockholm by the Principal and myself has gone well, and I have ordered a simulator, the journey there and back was stunning, with snow covered trees and fields with full grown deer stags just wandering around. The visit to the college by Jim and Linda went well and we have all been invited to one of the lecturer's homes for a meal tonight; one of the other lecturers is going to collect us.

Oh, my word, it is absolutely magical. The house is set to the right-hand side in a large fenced field, opposite on the left-hand side is a house that belongs to his wife's parents and directly to the left of us is a barn, which has a fully stocked bar in it. We are being led up the garden path to the main house and along the edges of the path set in the thick snow at equal distances are lit fire braziers. I have never seen anything so beautiful; it all looks like something out of a fairy tale.

We have all been handed an aperitif of cold tea, vodka, ice and pomegranate, it is delicious and very strong. We have then all been given a large beer. We are to eat a 'smorgasbord', which is a range of open sandwiches and delicacies, served as a buffet, jellied eels and eels prepared in other ways feature heavily. We are to fill our plates and then sit at the table. Before we can proceed to eat, we have to go to a triangular display unit which holds a vast array of small glasses, we then have to choose a glass and return to the table. I am sat with Jim, with Linda down the end of the table with a couple of the lecturers and the Principal on the opposite side of the table to Jim and me. These glasses are a bit tricky; they have a pointed bottom so that you cannot put them down on the table. The hostess has now come around the group with a basket of different flavoured tiny schnapps bottles, enough for one per person, so we have all chosen one. Jim and I do not know what we are supposed to do as we cannot put the glasses down, so we have poured the alcohol into the glasses and proceeded to drink it.

Wrong.

Oh dear, we were supposed to wait, so now the poor hostess has had to make a foray into the kitchen to find a large bottle of peach schnapps as all the little bottles have been chosen and has filled Jim and my glass again with the instructions to wait. What has ensued is a number of songs sung in Swedish, each song is sung and then a drink is taken from your glass, then another song, and another drink and so forth. Jim and I are slightly drunk.

The morning has gone well, the Principal and I joined the others at the college and because I am with the 'bigwig', we have been served the most enormous cream cake I have ever seen in my life with our coffee. Blimey, this is a challenge after all the schnapps last night.

We are now at the airport awaiting our return to the UK. Jim, Linda and myself have been and bought some souvenirs for family etc., whilst the Principal has retired to the bar. This has now caused me a massive headache as apart from the fact he has drunk numerous alcoholic drinks, he has become very awkward deciding to order food just when the call has been made for everyone to board the BA Airways plane home to Heathrow.

"Erm, I don't think you have got time for food," I have pointed out.

"Well, I am hungry," came the belligerent reply.

"Have something on the plane then," I reasoned.

"No, I want something here," was the response.

"Yes, well you should have ordered something earlier, shouldn't you? They have called for everyone to board the plane," I said like I was speaking to a child.

"Well, there's another one going in an hour," he stated with in a so-there manner, whilst pointing at the departure board.

"It's not a bloody bus!" I shouted in response.

I have had to practically manhandle him up out of this chair and point him in the direction of our departure gate, literally pushing him along with me chuntering on whilst they call out our particular names. Jim and Linda have followed in our wake with looks of absolute terror on their faces and if they think I am swapping my ticket this time with whoever has got the one sitting next to him, they have another think coming!

Monday 13 October 2008

I hope no one speaks to me because I do not think I can trust myself to answer, that function is not normally an issue for me but just now I do not think I would give anyone a coherent, reasonable response, no matter what the subject. I just cannot seem to get my brain in order, it is like it has had some sort of short circuit, but it must be fine because I am walking up this road in a normal manner. People are not staring at me and looking askance like I am mad or whispering behind their hands; in fact, they are going about their everyday business and completely ignoring me.

"If you get a chest pain before you receive an appointment, ring for an ambulance immediately," she said.

Was she talking to me?

Well, she must have been as there was only me in the room with her.

But that cannot be right, I honestly thought she would say that I was being silly, I was over reacting. I was some sort of closet hypochondriac.

It was not at that point on my zombie-like walk home, or when I reached my destination, that I realised it, but something had to change.

In the end, it's not the years in your life that count, it's the life in your years.

Abraham Lincoln

Monday 25 January 2010

I do not believe there are adequate words to describe leaving my adult children behind, even the expression adequate feels like a term that betrays the true depth of feeling in that moment. Some people will comment on the fact that they are 'adult' which should present the situation with a different perspective, that they had their own lives, that they were not being abandoned. The truth is that at that point of departure, I feel that is what they felt and as a mother no matter how rational or level headed I behaved, I felt it too. I will try to express how I felt but I honestly imagine whatever words I write to convey that sense of complete and utter loss will never truly reflect those feelings. I suppose you could compare it to grieving, but no one had died, to loss, but what had been forfeited, to defeat but what had been beaten?

The led up to the point of departure to our new life in France had been a melting pot of opposing or complimentary emotions, it seems a cliché to describe it thus, but that is exactly how it felt. The excitement at a new adventure, the quest to understand all the bureaucracy attached to buying a house in France. The painstaking, boring, methodical sorting of all possessions into coherent, identifiable assets, rubbish and purely personal but essential effects. Constant communication, written and oral for all existing, planned and future services balanced against the ball-breaking (ironic) male-chauvinistic attitude of French processes and procedures. The stress and worry of having to find nearly twenty-five thousand euros extra in agency and notaire fees, after the expressed pride and smugness in ourselves at being savvy, knowing, seasoned buyers, to the endless dump runs and charity donations that could have generated some supporting funds if we had planned things better.

All this noise amidst a non-acknowledgement of any personal or emotional effect this process may be having internally on me or on any family member around. Until the inevitable explosion of pent-up anger, betrayal and incomprehension led to an all-out, no holds barred screaming, shouting, sobbing, expulsion of passion and emotion.

It is strange to reflect that although there were a multitude of words spoken, screamed or shouted and a host of conflicting and wide-ranging emotions expressed, not once did any of us say what was really at the bottom of it all. As a family, our best form of defence is to attack, that is our modus operandi and to be fair, I was always trying to display a positive façade. It was easy to do so when people were joining in the overall excitement and exclaiming such reinforcing sentiments such as, 'oh, I wish we could do that', 'I've always wanted to live abroad', 'how lucky you are' and 'how exciting', it was easy to go along with the supportive encouraging statements. It was not until a family member not within the cauldron of passions, who professed 'not to be very good at this' said 'We will miss you' did the wall I had built and was hidden behind come tumbling down.

Norfolk N Good

Wells Next the Sea 5 December 2013

Risk of loss of life!

Not what you want to hear at five thirty in the morning via an automated phone call.

I have listened to the message five times now, partly because I rushed downstairs after being woken from my slumber to get to the phone only for me to miss the call and equally because I cannot comprehend correctly what it is telling me.

We have only been here three days; how can this be happening?

Mr C is not even here, he has stayed overnight in Ipswich with work. What is it saying to me?

I have listened to it again several times and I think I have got the gist: there is going to be a sea surge at high tide tonight and they are going to close the roads at four o'clock this afternoon and I need to evacuate because my life is in danger.

What?

We are renting a furnished house in Wells Next the Sea, just off Staithe Street for six months over the winter period; our main home is now in France. Mr C's mum lives in Norwich and has had her hip replaced and we are here to try to help and support her—not physically of course. Wells is thirty-five miles away from Norwich and the invalid, but this is the only house that is available to rent that is furnished and will accommodate us, two dogs and a cat. That is a lie actually, there was another one at Sea Palling, but it is in the middle of nowhere, very difficult for Mr C to get to work and I would be totally isolated seeing that I do not drive.

What to do?

I really need to ring the owner of the house who lives in London, but it is only six thirty in the morning, I will try and wait as long as I can before I ring.

I have managed to wait until eight o'clock but I am that stressed I really do need to speak to her.

The phone is ringing at the other end and Sally has picked up, thank goodness and said a sleepy, "Hello."

"Oh hello, Sally, I am so sorry to ring you so early in the morning but I have received an automated message about a sea surge that's going to happen this evening," I blurted out at breakneck speed.

"Oh," came the response.

"Yes, and I don't know what to do. Do I go and get some sand bags from somewhere or something?" I questioned a little high pitched I have to say. I have never had a house so close to the sea before and I am not a natural with nautical affairs with hailing from Oldham.

"No, there's no need," she replied a little dismissively, I have to say.

"Well, they are saying there is a risk of loss of life," I screeched in a 'so there' voice.

She started to laugh and said, "You don't need to worry."

What is wrong with the woman? I am telling her that 'these people' whoever they are seem quite adamant that there is a big problem and she is chuckling at me.

"Yes, but the sea may get into your house," I responded triumphantly.

She laughed again and said in a 'you, stupid woman' mode, "They have only sent that message to me because I am on the committee, it won't get up there, it's fine," and with that said her farewells and put the phone down.

Well, that is okay for her to say that, and if I may add a bit blasé, but that message has really freaked me out. I cannot seem to focus on anything else or think straight. It says 'risk of loss of life' and that they are closing the roads and people should evacuate, for goodness' sake. Oh god, what a day, what shall I do?

I have decided to ring Mr C to see what he thinks.

"Morning, love," came the normal reply from Mr C, nothing today is normal, "you're up early."

No shit sherlock.

"I have been up since five thirty actually," I replied a little shirtily I have to say.

"Has one of the dogs been playing up?" He enquired.

"No, they have not! I have received an automated message from some committee telling me that there is going to be a sea surge tonight, we need to evacuate and there is risk of loss of life!" I blurted out at speed and a little high pitched.

"Oh," came the response.

"Oh?" I replied incredulously. "I have spoken to Sally and she says it will be okay, how does she know?" I screeched, "They are saying to evacuate and loss of life!"

"Oh," he said again.

"Will you stop keep saying, Oh," I stated exasperated, "they are closing the roads at four o'clock this afternoon so you are going to have to come and get me."

"But I am in a meeting at that time," came the reply.

It has taken me a little while to digest this response I have to say; I cannot get my head around the sheer nonchalance of his reply when I have just told him my life is at risk. I am totally nonplussed but now I am seriously angry.

"What?" I bellowed, "You get here this afternoon and collect me and the dogs!" I screamed; an order rather than a request. Bloody Hell!

What is the matter with people? They just do not seem to take me seriously.

Mr C has arrived and we have put Steve, the cat in the top room in the house on the third floor with enough food for a couple of days and his litter tray. He will be safe up there, if the sea gets in, although Sally does not think it will. Well, I may not be an expert on all things marine but I believe you can argue with some things but the sea is not one of them, so I am taking no chances.

We are taking the dogs with us to a Premier Inn in Norwich; they cannot stay in the hotel though, they will have to sleep in the car, but at least they will not drown.

I know some people may think that I am overreacting but I have experienced something similar to this at home in France.

The eastward-moving Atlantic storm dubbed 'Xynthia' left devastation in its wake as it passed through western Europe at the weekend, leaving dozens dead and half a million without electricity.

In France, we live twenty-five minutes by car from the coast and we could clearly hear the sea roaring. It was impossible to sleep and I just lay there thinking, *'Well this house has stood for one hundred and fifty years, so hopefully it should be fine, and it is.'* Unfortunately, that was not the case for many others.

President Nicolas Sarkozy visited L'Aiguillon-sur-Mer on Monday, where he mourned, "A national catastrophe, a human drama with a dreadful toll," and said, "the urgent thing is to support the families who have people missing or dead." Sarkozy unveiled three million euros of emergency funds available for the victims and promised that electricity would be restored by Tuesday.

L'Aiguillon-sur-Mer is just down the coast from our house and the poor inhabitants there bore the brunt of the storm, the sea wall protecting the town was destroyed, so the water rose quickly as the people slept and they drowned in their sleep. Those poor people, there were over fifty souls who died. The majority of the houses in the region are single bungalows and many are fitted with electric shutters for extra security; unfortunately, this quest for safety proved fatal. As the sea rose and swiftly entered the homes, those people who were not killed in their beds tried to escape but the electricity shorted the shutters and so could not be opened so they frantically tried to reach the loft space in the roof but their efforts in a lot of cases were hopeless and they drowned.

I did not sign up for that. I never in all the planning and preparation believed that after a month of living in France, there would be a cyclone that triggered a mini tsunami.

We were so lucky, those poor people were not, so it is hardly surprising that I feared history was repeating itself and somehow, I was the catalyst. I know that is stupid superstition to think like that but after a month of living in France, they had a cyclone and three days after living here, there is a sea surge.

6 December

Carnage!

Charlie Hall, Deputy Chief Constable of Norfolk; "In places, water levels were higher than those experienced in the flooding of 1953, when many people lost their lives. Thankfully, that has not been the case on this occasion because of a combination of improved defences in place and the concerted efforts of the community, the emergency services and the agencies that have worked to support the evacuation and keep people informed."

I do not know if this speech will do anything for the poor people who have lost their homes.

Sally was right, the sea did not get into her house and the cat was fine, but it did get part way up the road and flooded the shops and The Golden Fleece Pub at the bottom of Staithe Street and the Quayside. The schooner, The Albatross, nearly landed in Platten's Fish and Chip Shop.

9 December

Oh, my god, I have just nearly caused an international incident televised on all the major TV channels!

I say 'I' who I really mean is 'Jack' the West Highland White.

The house we are renting has a tiny garden and is unfortunately shared with the holiday home at right angles to this abode. I have been told by Sally, the owner of our house that the people next door are from Cambridge and visit infrequently and as we have only been here a week, we have not yet seen them. The problem is that there are no gates on one side of the garden and two exuberant Westies will find the thought of escape and adventures too much of an opportunity to miss. Plus, it is not nice if you come on your holidays and the first thing you see are two dogs doing their ablutions outside your kitchen window. Consequently, as soon as I have had my first morning coffee, I am dressed and out of the door with two excitable and desperate canines.

We have not got into the swing of things really because of the sea surge and the fact we have only been here a short while. However, there are three things that have become consistent in that short time, the path we take, the eagerness of the dogs to be at a certain point on that route to do their 'businesses' and the penchant for Jack to want to have an altercation with any person or animal he feels worthy of his attention.

Thus, we have arrived at the bottom of Staithe Street which is just around the corner from the house ready to cross to the car park, then onto the quay path, past the custom house and so towards the lifeboat station and ultimately the beach.

Jack has gone a bit berserk it has to be said because instead of the usual couple of victims for his ire, there seem to be a lot of men and women in formal suits and earphones just waiting for his challenge, it is a bit strange. Further weirdness has been revealed as I have turned left at the corner onto The Quay.

Wow! What is going on?

In and around The Port of Wells car parks are a multitude of people, further black-suited individuals who I have come to realise are some kind of bodyguard, policemen men and women, people sat in official and unofficial looking cars, curious locals, SKY TV vans, with presenters talking to camera, BBC, ITV and other channels performing the same procedure and me and two dogs.

Too late, I have apprehended the danger of my situation.

As I have walked, I have to say a little dumbfounded by the amount of people, Jack has ceased his murderous foray into unsuspecting victims and has decided that he has reached the point where he needs to perform the function for which this walk is intended.

Oh please, God, no!

I have never been so embarrassed in all my life; well I am sure I have been but it does not feel so at the moment. I have changed route and hurriedly bundled myself and the boys around the corner onto Beach Road where hopefully no one can see us.

Wrong.

There is a black-suited man sat in a very official car in absolute stiches at me and I have to admit that I have succumbed to a fit of the giggles myself.

Jack has just done a pooh in front of the nation's TV Channels who are awaiting the arrival of David Cameron.

David Cameron says more could be done to prevent floods, "I think you can always do more, so here we are with a flood that was bigger than 1953, but with many fewer homes flooded—even though of course, we have built lots of homes in flood plains since them.

So, I think the figure is had there been no flood defences, you could have seen 800,000 homes flooded. So, there's always more that can be done.

There's always more flood defences that can be put in place, the funding is there but you can't always protect everything."

January 1 2014

I am absolutely shattered and slightly hungover.

We have had all the kids and grandchildren to stay, that is not entirely true, James and his family have not been this weekend but came for the Wells Christmas Tide earlier in December. It has been a bit of a challenge for the organisers of the festival who were determined they were not going to be beaten after the previous weekend's tidal surge. It was brilliant, Staithe Street was closed to pedestrians and a multitude of stalls were erected from mulled cider to gift stalls. Hundreds of people, including us, stood on the quay side awaiting Santa who was arriving by boat and he was welcomed in by Singing Elves, donkey 'reindeers' (they wore felt antler ears), fire twirlers and drummers followed by extremely noisy and showy fireworks—marvellous!

So, they have all gone now, we had Jessie and Mark and their brood in the top bedroom, Daphne and Luke and their brood in the front bedroom, Jemima, Cecil and the dog in the back bedroom, Graham and Suzy in the lounge, Steve the cat in the kitchen, Mr C, Jack, Harry and me in the dining room.

We had a treasure hunt, guess the items on a tray, pop a balloon with your bottom and eat hula hoops off a rope without using your hands and copious amounts of alcohol for the adults. They were in teams of two and Jemima and Zach won, I need a lie down in a dark room now.

Life has carried on in a regular routine, commencing with the early morning dog walk. We have not had a repeat of the all humiliation pooping session on live TV but one thing is constant, Jack's unchanging love of the beautiful white Alsatian bitch we meet on our walks.

She, on the other hand, remains aloof, impervious to his advances and does not even give him eye contact, which is a bit difficult anyway seeing as he only comes up to her kneecaps. She just walks past maintaining that beautiful, elegant behaviour whilst he howls like a banshee. His conduct however, is getting worse; I know he is not used to being in a town and normally at home in France, it is only the fishermen at the lake he harasses mainly because they are usually the only people, he meets but here it is a different kettle of fish. So, I have resorted to buying them both a citronella dog collar, poor Harry, he does not deserve it as he is as good as gold, but I do not want to treat them differently, bonkers I know. Anyway, it has not worked. The idea is that if the dog barks, a spray of citronella is squirted in their face. I thought that it was a good idea as back in France when we have visitors who Jack does not like, well there is only one really, Sabine; I resort to squirting water at him from a washing up bottle which does shut him up, so I thought this would work.

Wrong.

Unfortunately, when he has barked, it has squirted him as it should, but then indignantly, he has barked back at it which has resulted in it squirting again. At this point, Harry has become involved because they both walk together and will not be parted and so it has squirted Harry in the face also. He has become indignant and so barked back. It has now become a bit of a barking game which they are apparently enjoying a lot, each taking it in turn to bark and so are both absolutely drenched wet through. Well, they will not get any mosquitos biting them that is for sure.

I have decided for the peace of mind of everyone, including me, that I would change tack and have been up to the pet shop on Staithe Street and bought a collar just for Jack. Poor Harry gets dragged into this and it is not his fault, so he has been left out of this particular experiment. The collar I have bought, the lady assures me is just what Jack and I need. It is a dog training and walking collar which fits around the nose. It has taken a considerable amount of ingenuity on my part to get the damn thing on Jack, he is not happy and we have set off on a trial walk with Harry on his normal lead in the opposite direction to the normal route to see how we go.

It has not gone well.

I am now laid full length on the floor in the middle of Standard Road in front of the Chandlery shop, Harry is sat politely at the side of my head and Jack who is now wearing the collar like a dicky bow underneath his chin is stood at the side of my feet barking.

I have returned to normal leads because it is better the devil you know.

Steve, the cat has had issues whilst he is here also. In France, he is an outside cat, but as he is deaf and I have to say a bit daft, he has had to become an inside cat whilst he is here which he seems okay with.

Wrong.

I have just returned back from the normal morning dog walk utilising the usual leads when something has struck me, figuratively speaking, not physically as I have entered back into the dining room through the only outside door.

Oh, you can tell this used to be a pub because it smells of beer. The owners bought the house many years ago and have renovated it and during that exercise found out it used to be a hostelry and it still has the wooden doors into the cellar that the beer barrels were rolled down. However, it is not beer I can smell but another type of alcohol.

The house is fully furnished and in the massive fireplace which no longer functions as a heating source is a lovely old set of drawers. On top of this piece of furniture, I have added a wine rack full of bottles of red and rose vino. It is no longer completely full. Steve the cat exploring whilst we were out has located a chimney above the wine rack and attempted unsuccessfully to climb the two-floor height smoke stack in an attempt to reach the small shaft of daylight at the top and therefore freedom.

Steve who is normally pure white is now black, covered in soot and has most, if not all his claws missing which are strewn around the flag hearth. Also dispersed around the flag dining room floor are the smashed remains and contents of several bottles of wine—what a waste.

Since we have been here, we have had other visitors who have come to see us who hail from where we live in France, including Emmanuelle from the shop and has a holiday home in Norfolk and Bill and Becky who have a holiday home in France and a permanent home near Birmingham. Bill and Becky are staying at a bed and breakfast place in Wells and we have just met them in the Edinburgh pub at the top of Staithe Street. I know this is a massive generalisation but there appears to be two types of people in Wells Next the Sea (the kids keep adding a 'to' when telling people where we live now). The first set are the visitors who have second homes here who tend to frequent places like The Globe Inn on The Buttlands or the Yacht Club and the second set who are the locals who frequent places like The Edinburgh where we are now.

That was interesting.

We have had many a good night here, meeting various locals, including ones that we recognise but do not know their names and the mad cat woman (not my description) and her Maths teacher boyfriend who got very friendly with us. Tonight, with Bill and Becky, we have encountered the Polish Farm workers again, one of who took a shine to Bill and wanted him to drink a shot she had bought him. We have managed to avoid a tense situation, Becky was not too impressed by the young women's advances towards her husband and Bill did not want to drink the shot, whether he did not like the look of it or in deference to his wife, so I have drunk the damn thing. This, it appears was an acceptable compromise for all involved.

March 2014

We have got the house until May but I have decided to return home to France earlier for several reasons; firstly, because the weather is so much better there but secondly, for a much deeper reason. North Norfolk has made me want to return to my first love—writing. I do not know why but something about living here as given me the impetus to start again, well I do, it is linked to my mum.

On the day of my mum's funeral all those years ago when I was twelve, I was not allowed to go with the rest of the family; I had to go to school as usual and then go to my friend at the Albion Pub. I cannot remember a single thing about that day, how I felt at school, what time I went to her house, what time I went home, nothing. I think I just blocked it from my memory because it was too painful. My overall feeling on reflection is that they should have let me go with them to the funeral.

It was no surprise that after my mum died, my dad frequented a lot more of the pubs that featured in our lives more than he did before, or that is how it appeared to me. He had always played darts and crib when my mum was alive but afterwards, he just seemed to want to live in the pubs or maybe it was that I noticed it more because it was just me and him without my mum; there as a smoke screen between the two of us. Before I had not needed to wonder where he was, what he was doing, that was what my mum did. To be honest, I had never sat down to talk to him before, me and my brother had tea together and then my mum and dad later. I had absolutely no adult conversation; I did not know about politics, what was happening in the world or what was even happening on our street. It was no wonder he wanted grown-up conversation, I was twelve and my main focus was playing two-ball on the kitchen wall.

Mum had been my guiding light. She was my reference point, my main stay. I could not figure out what I was going to do without her. The pain I felt inside was so deep, there seemed to be no end. Some people when trying to explain what it feels like to give birth say that if you took your top lip, stretched it over your head, pulled it down your back and then stood on it then that would be it or near enough. The pain I had was a dulled version of that all around my heart and it was relentless. The truth was I missed her; I missed her So much. All the conformity, the comforting normality went out of my life to be replaced by a kind of organised chaos, well not that organised really. My eldest sister had her husband and their children, my other sister had her husband and their daughter, my brother had his girlfriend and who did I have? I had my dad!

So, that is where the writing started; it was like an escape, something that helped me try to make sense of the situation. My poor friend at the pub used to be held captive in the front room with me whilst I read the torrid love stories I had written. There was no coincidence that these stories always had unrequited love in them, a change of heart by the intended recipient of that adoration and a sad ending where he died before they could be together. Unfortunately, these stories were inflicted on my poor friend on a regular basis until my father himself died and I stopped writing altogether.

Something here has made me want to start again, so I am returning to France to start to write a book after first saying goodbye to Mr C's mother.

We have come to Mr C's mum's house in Norwich, she has recovered enough for me to leave; not that I have done that much whilst I have been here to be honest, she is a very independent person. Mr C will stay until May. She is what some people would call a 'difficult woman', I just think she is a right madam. She is very astute and identifies your buttons almost immediately, she definitely knows what mine are.

However, she normally leaves mine alone and concentrates on Mr and his weight but today she seems to be concentrating on someone else until Mr C went upstairs to the loo.

"You are looking well," she has commented silkily.

"Yes, I'm good, thanks," I replied a little warily.

"Yes, Mr C looks to have lost some weight," comes the response, oh this is a new tack.

"Erm, I don't know," I said, I do know and there is no way he has lost weight is what I thought.

"Mmmm and you look to have put weight on," commented the madam.

"Erm, I don't think so," I replied trying not to laugh.

"Yes, I think so, Mr C has lost all the weight and you have put it on." She is a monkey.

"Erm, I don't think so," I responded, that was all I could think of to say.

She looked me straight in the eye and said, "Well, never mind, you are happy with your big, fat, round face!"

Today is the last viewing of the house we are renting before I return to France. Sally has put the house on the market and as part of the rental agreement, we consented to let the Estate Agents, Sowerbys, show around any prospective buyers. This has not been an issue and there have been a couple of viewings but no offers as yet. Prospective buyers of the property are normally shown around by Jo or Jeremy who know the layout well, I normally sit with the dogs in the lounge; however, as the boys are very nosey, they do try to accompany everyone around the house. Today, however, the lady showing the house, Ann, has never been before and keeps asking me for my help over certain aspects but there are some of the details I do not know as I have only been here four months and it is not my house.

"How much a week do you get for renting it out in the holiday season?" The prospective lady buyer has enquired.

"Oh sorry, I don't know that as it is not my house and we are only renting for six months," I have responded smiling at her.

She is not smiling at me, in fact, she is looking at me as if I am something she has found on the bottom of her shoe, "How much a week do you get for renting it out when not in the holiday season?" She has responded.

Is she deaf?

"Erm, I don't know, as I said earlier, this is not my house, so no I have not got a clue whether it is rented out weekly or what the price would be if it was," I replied.

"Oh, do you rent it out monthly in the holiday season then?" She persisted.

She is getting a tad on my nerves now, she is one of those entitled people that visit around here, that believe they are better than other people and should get what they want and now. She has probably got a couple of feral children running around somewhere dressed in multi-coloured and mismatched patterned clothes whist wearing wellingtons.

"The owner does do bed and breakfast and I have a sheet with the prices on if you want to see it," I am trying to be helpful even if she is being a trifle superior in her manner. Ann, the estate agent is looking a little uncomfortable.

"Oh, okay, but I really wanted to know about short-term rental prices," she stated.

Well, you may want to but there are only so many ways I can tell you that I do not know what the prices are is what I thought but what I actually said probably a little directly, "Do you want to know what we pay a month? I can tell you that."

This seemed to satisfy her, although you could not tell that from her demeanour, and she then started on a different tack, "Can we look in the cellar?" No pleases or anything like that.

"I am sorry the door has been locked by the owner," I will be glad when she has gone.

"Well, have you got the key?" Was the curt response.

"No, I have not," I nearly screeched, what is wrong with the woman?

"Well how big is it?" she enquired.

I think there is something wrong with her. "Sorry, no, I don't know how big it is, as I have already said, the owner has locked it and I have not been in," I said slightly screechy.

"Well, can I fit my canoe in it?" she questioned.

I have stared at her for some considerable time, quite dumbfounded I have to say. How many times can I tell her the same thing over and over again and to be perfectly honest, I have never measured a canoe in my life and even if I had, it would be completely redundant as the door is locked.

"As I have said on several occasions, this is not my house and quite frankly I don't know how big your canoe is!" was my considered and sarcastic response. My suggestion that she could put her canoe in the outside toilet in the garden has not been received well. She has now left and taken her waspish and well-spoken face with her.

Sorry, Sally, but I do not think she will be making an offer.

Slow You Down

Cromer February 2019

Who would have thought we would end up back in Norfolk and for good?

When we came back from France to live permanently in the UK, in 2014, we moved into a bungalow in Chesterfield to be near four of our children and all the grandchildren. We felt that as that would be the last house we owned, we should plan for the future and get a home all on one level.

Wrong.

It was on all one level, that was correct, but it was just not right for us, we did not feel old enough to live there. Although we modernised the house, it was the demographics of the area, everyone seemed to be in bed by six at night. We decided we wanted a house with an actual upstairs, although it had been fun watching two of the grandchildren searching all over the bungalow to locate a staircase. We also wanted to be in a place where the lifestyle was like France and close enough for all the kids to visit us without having to use a passport and a day to get to us. As it was definitely going to be our last house, I wanted to follow the dream of living near the sea, I had got the bug when we lived in Wells Next the Sea. North Norfolk seemed to offer us that lifestyle, people said hello to you in the street for a start, and after a house-hunting expedition, we bought a home in Cromer.

Before we moved to Cromer, we said that once the furniture was in the house, we would go into the town and do two things.

Firstly, we would have a drink at the Hotel de Paris, in recognition of Mr C's dad who passed away in 2006; he worked for the Post Office and used to organise the Christmas party on behalf of the benevolent fund which was held each year at the hotel.

We have just left the hotel and had a look at the sea at which point I have got very emotional because I never thought I would live here. Afterwards, we moved onto the NO1 Fish Restaurant. The second thing we said would do was have fish and chips for our first tea, living at the seaside.

We have just perused the menu and the manager, I think that is who he is, has just come along to take our order and upon hearing my accent has immediately said, "I bet I know what you want."

I was a little taken aback, partly, because I am tired after spending two full days to move house and secondly, because I could not fathom why he would know what I wanted, so I just uttered a little, "Oh?"

"Yes, you will want a fish finger sandwich!" He replied triumphantly.

At first, I have regarded him with confusion and then the penny has dropped; it is my northern accent, cheeky bugger. What I wanted to say to him was, no I want lobster actually, but what I did say was, "No, thank you, I will have fish and chips please," partly, because they did not have lobster on the menu and partly, because I am not as rude as he is.

We love it here and even though the egg man has shouted after me in a very strong Norfolk accent as I have crossed the carpark, "Look at her!" he bellowed to all and sundry, "she's that little, I bet she can't get up the stairs." I already feel like I belong, even with my northern accent.

After our first foray into Cromer nightlife, we decided that we would go to the Greek restaurant that everyone was raving about. This raving was through comments on the internet as we do not know any actual people yet as we have only been here a couple of weeks and we are literally living in the middle of a building site. The thing is although we are permeant residents here, we are behaving as if we are on holiday all the time, gin and tonic on the pier, fish and chips, willy-nilly and red wine and peanuts in the pubs.

Constantia Cottage Restaurant is in East Runton, which is still part of Cromer and just down the coast a little way. The restaurant was bought in 1980 by the current owners, it seats up to one hundred people and apparently Greek music is played by their son's band, the Constantia Brothers. As it is only February and out of season, ooh look at me, I am already a seasoned seaside person, we do not think there would be any live music. We had meant to go on Saturday but for some reason we cancelled and moved the booking to tonight, Tuesday.

We do not know where to park as we have never been here before and did not know whether we should leave the car on the street in front of the main entrance. However, we have found the car park around the back; it is a bit worrying as we are the only car in it. After careful consideration, we have decided to enter through the door leading from the car park, we have gone through our usual barging and pushing each other when going somewhere we do not know while saying,

"You go first!"

"No, you go first!"

So, we have bundled into a long corridor with myself in the lead.

To the left of the long thin corridor are two doors marked 'Ladies' and 'Gents' and further along is a wide opening to the right with what appears to be the kitchen at the very end of the hallway, I can hear talking and the side view of what I believe to be a man's leg.

We are creeping along the hallway towards the opening on the right, looking around us like a startled deer not unlike the Muntjacs that are all around Cromer and we are whispering. Why? I have no idea. On entering through the opening, it has revealed a large empty dining room with trestle tables all set for dinner and to the right along the full length of the wall is a stage with an array of different musical instruments and chairs and stools. Facing the stage and to the left is a small opening which we have made our way to and this has revealed a much smaller dining room which is also empty.

"Come on, lets' go, this is not looking very promising," whispered Mr C.

"Okay," I have whispered back.

We have both turned around to be met by a smiling gentleman wearing a waiter's uniform, he looks to be in his early seventies and is obviously the owner of the leg I saw. He has rushed forward making his greetings to us both and has kissed me. This has totally startled me; I was used to being kissed on both cheeks when we lived in France but not since we moved back to the UK, but he is Mediterranean, of course. He has led us through the smaller dining room towards another opening on the left wall of that room, while Mr C is uttering under his breath, "Oh God, we have got to stay now."

Our waiter has uttered the words, "So, this is the bar, what would you like to drink?"

It has taken us both sometime to answer, I have never seen a bar quite like it.

To the left is the said bar, with drinks etc. as you would expect and around the square room are several round wooden tables and chairs. The walls are completely covered with memorabilia of what I determined to be The Constantia Brothers, joined by their sister and other random celebrities from the 1980s such as Michael Barrymore and the like; I presume these were appearing on the pier at the theatre and had come here to eat. In the middle of the room are two battered cream leather sofas and a coffee table, to which myself and Mr C have been led, it feels like we are guests of honour. Our drinks of red wine have been produced, which taste very dusty to me and a bowl of cheese shape biscuit snacks. The only other people in the room besides ourselves and the waiter are a couple sat at one of the tables over near the window. We have smiled and said hello, while he has nodded and she has just looked at us like she is chewing a wasp and neither of them have said a word.

I am struggling very hard not to go off into hysterics while drinking my dusty wine and just as I thought I was going to lose it; light relief has been presented by three new people that have arrived.

These have been seated at one of the tables, and have said hello to us and started talking, they appear to be locals, a man, lady and their grown-up daughter who is a teacher.

All of a sudden, the waiter has appeared and asked us to go through to have our meal, we have all been shown to our allocated tables, there are seven of us in total; I really do not think we needed to book. The waiter has come over to take our order and has started the process with, "Oh, you are in for a real treat tonight, it is the main man my dad who is the chef tonight."

What?

He must be ninety if he is a day if he is this man's dad, but I replied with a noncommittal 'oh', because to be honest, I am at a loss at what else to say.

We have eaten our starter and main course mainly in silence, partly because everyone can hear everyone else's conversations and partly because we thought the food would be wonderful, but to be honest, it is a bit greasy or that may be how it was supposed to be.

The waiter has asked us if we enjoyed our meal and of course we have said, "Yes," very English and then asked if we would like dessert. It appears there is only one choice for our delectation and that is Baclava, which is at this moment being wheeled out on a gold hostess trolley by the waiter's mum. I have nearly lost it, but I have managed to keep it together, decline dessert, pay the bill and made our hopefully polite if speedy exit. It was just like being in the middle of the television sketch 'two soups'.

Cromer 9 March 2020

The last six weeks have been some of the hardest in my life.

Mrs C's mum is still with us, she is in her nineties and her body and mind are fading fast, her tongue however, is not.

Up until December, things were bad but manageable; we have moved to Cromer partly to be near her and to somehow help; oh my God, that is an understatement. She was having carers going in four times a day, but being the feisty woman she is, and who can blame her, when they arrived to get her out of bed, wash her and dress her, she would be downstairs in her chair fully dressed. Good for her. This state of affairs with her mobility issues though could not be sustained and during December and the first ten days of January, the ambulance has been called to her home seven times.

It always followed the same process, she would fall (actually, she never fell, she just slipped), she would press the button on the necklace around her neck which would alert the response team. They in turn would try and telephone her, but she could not get to the phone and so they would call Mr C's sister who lived nearby to go and check on her. This never happened as Mr C's sister would say there was no way she could possibly get round there and would call an ambulance. The ambulance would arrive and access the house using the key lock system and try and persuade the 'slipper' to go to the hospital. Unfortunately, the invalid would not go and they could not make her, she is in a stage in her life were all care is palliative and although she has dementia, she is not deemed a danger to herself. This meant that nothing could be done unless she had a broken bone or a blood pressure issue or some such thing, but as none of these conditions presented themselves, they were powerless to do anything other than pick her up and put her back in bed or wherever.

So, this process is repeated each time.

I kept asking Mr C's sister, "Why don't the responders ring us, we can come from Cromer and put her back in bed?" But no answer was forthcoming, it turns out that Mr C's name and contact details had not been included in any documentation at all, it is as if he does not exist.

As this information was not revealed until much later down the line, I was completely baffled and could only speculate at the cost of these regular ambulance call outs and which poor people with a real need were being left waiting whilst they picked 'madam' up off the floor.

On the last and final callout, the invalid had a blood pressure issue and so they whisked her off to hospital and she could not block the visit.

At this point, two things occurred simultaneously, it became quite obvious that Mr C's mum could not return home and Mr C's sister stated that she 'was having nothing more to do with it and it was now down to us, she had done her bit'. It may be just a coincidence that now things have become very difficult that she has decided to retreat.

At first, we visited the hospital regularly and when she was being lucid, she could see that she could not return home and asked us to look at a care home which one of the other patients had mentioned. Which we did. It was like a hotel, with a 'restaurant', a 'bar', a 'gym' and an array of other facilities, it also cost two thousand pounds a week to live there!

Then to make things even harder, the ward got Novovirus and was closed down for four weeks. This had a specific and repeatable effect on the invalid. She was now isolated with no visitors and the only way to vent her frustration was to speak to her daughter each day, she had had a conversation with her every day for the last at least thirty years at least.

Oh, my God.

This would always end with the same result, further frustration and anger on behalf of the invalid as Mr C's sister told her to speak to me as she had no idea what was going on. Mr C's sister would then ring me every day after this mother and daughter call to get an update on what was going on and to complain about her mother.

I in turn would then receive a call from the totally frustrated invalid telling me that if I did not 'get her out of there', she would call the police.

And so, it continued until one day the hospital rang Mr C's sister to say they were sending the invalid home; we still did not exist on any documentation. I was then called by Mr C's sister and I in turn called the hospital.

What ensued was a completely frustrating conversation with the ward culminating with me uttering the words 'safeguarding issue' and the hospital terminating the conversation immediately as I was not a blood relative.

I was livid! Mr C could not deal with day-to-day events as he was identified as a 'key worker' and worked away from home four days a week and Mr C's sister would not deal with the situation. That only left me, but now I was persona non grata because I was only related by marriage.

I managed to locate Mr C and a subsequent phone call from him initiated a visit from the relevant department representatives and the invalid was deemed incapable of looking after herself physically and mentally. The social care system was then in charge; she was assigned a social worker and so she had to go in a care home permanently. As the hospital needed the bed for people, they could cure, the social worker Lorraine found her a temporary home.

Oh, my God.

As Mr C's mum owns her own home, it meant two things, she has to pay for her own care and she has to find her own place to live, which in reality that meant me.

What ensued was a complete nightmare. I spent hours and hours every single day searching the internet for care homes within a certain price bracket that indeed had a bed that was available and if they had a bed available that were they willing to assess the invalid. It became a career. Whilst this process was taking place, I was receiving daily calls from Mr C's sister complaining about the once-a-week thirty-minute journey to visit her mum (it took us one hour and ten minutes), asking every time why she was in that home and why could she not be in one nearer to them (because this was the only one available), asking for a detailed update but then telling her mother she knew nothing. Whilst this was happening, the mum and daughter were speaking daily, whereupon after each call Mr C's mum would call to rant and rave at me, telling me she would change her will and I would not get a penny (I am not even in the will) and constantly saying she was going to ring the police. I was the only one who could calm her down and this I had to do every day.

Eventually, we found her somewhere at seven hundred and eighty pounds per week, which was one of the cheapest. We did look at other places which would result in me being in tears when leaving uttering, "I would not put a dead dog in there."

Cromer 23 March 2020

We are in lockdown!

Not something I ever thought I would say, in fact 'lockdown' is not a word I have ever had in my vocabulary. We are in a Global Pandemic, Coronavirus, or COVID-19 as it is known.

Noah our grandson was terrified because he thought it was Cromervirus and his 'nana' lived in Cromer and therefore we were in the epicentre of the pandemic.

The care home Mr C's mum is in has closed access to all relatives and so we had a week when we could see her and now consequently, she is isolated again.

Everyone including us are now isolated too.

Cromer 26 May 2020

Mr C's mum passed away today, on her own in hospital, a consultant held her hand at her last moments.

Cromer June 2020

We have just had Mr C's mum's funeral, no wake due to restrictions, there were ten mourners.

Cromer July 2020

Have you ever tried to clear and sell a house in a pandemic?

Oh, my word.

It is completely draining, practically, physically and emotionally and because I had taken on the lion's share because of Mr C's key worker status, mentally exhausting for me. On top of the whole, hospital, care homes, mother and daughter dynamics, dealing with the funeral directors, the crematorium, the vicar, the internment and a whole lot more, I have gained skills that I do not believe I will need again in my lifetime, hopefully, but consequently I am spent.

To try and escape the mental exhaustion and to divert my thoughts in a positive direction, I have decided to finish my novel. I had started writing it after I had returned to France after staying in Wells Next the Sea, but stopped because life got in the way. After returning to live in the UK, grandchildren consumed my days and when we eventually moved here, it went on the back burner to exploring. Once the lockdown and all the emotionally draining incidents arrived, I gained the impetus to finish it. Some people may think that that would be the last thing you would do, but I feel it is intrinsically linked to why I write in the first place and the person I have become.

Why write a book?

Have you ever had something in your head, a thought or a notion that was just out of reach? That you just could not quite get hold of, no matter how hard you tried? That you knew was there, lurking, but every time you tried to grasp hold of the end of it, it was like when you played 'What time is it, Mr Wolf?' When you turned around to grab your friend you just missed the back of her jumper. That is what it was like when I started to write.

Why write a book? Many people have asked me this question with varying levels of incredulity, cynicism and downright dismissal. So, why?

To be honest, my desire to write started to formulate as an idea for one reason only, but was eventually because of something a lot stronger. Initially, it was because there were so many events in my life which were occurring which seemed to be slightly unusual to say the least. Each time one of these events would occur, I would say, "Well, I would write a book but no one would believe me!" So, the seed was sown. The real reason was deeper than that though and inexplicably linked with this thought in my head, but it was not a thought it was a tune, a song, a ditty or something, I just could not quite grasp what it was.

It was in there and just came out every now and again, why? I do not know, but it would be there one minute and gone the next, always just out of reach. I do not know when it actually started popping up in there but it reached a peak in my early forties. I could actually hum a few bars and I would do so to anyone who cared to listen, trying to find out what the damn tune was. Maybe I was not humming it to the right people or maybe my talent for humming in tune was a bit dubious because no-one ever knew what it was until one day it popped in there again and I hummed it to Mr C. By some miracle, he said that he knew it, which is strange in itself because he cannot normally recognise a tune to save his life. Well, he did not so much know it but he knew where it came from, it was from 'Madame Butterfly'. Oh.

I had never been to an Opera in my life at that point and could not understand why it was in there, in my head, but Mr C as ever recognised something within me that needed dealing with and bought tickets for the show in Sheffield. Mr C could not go with me, (thank God, he said) so I took my daughter Daphne. I have never, ever, before or ever since experienced anything like it. I was emotional anyway for some unknown reason but when the song, the actual tune was sung, it was like having some kind of religious experience. I started to cry uncontrollably, I had goose pimples from the top of my head to the tip of my toes and every hair on my body was stood to attention. By the end of the song, I was sobbing like a baby and I did not care who knew it. I still did not know what the damn thing was called.

I was on the phone to my eldest sister a couple of days later and during the usual oh what have you been doing type conversation, I mentioned that I had been to see Madame Butterfly. "Oh. Yes," she said breathlessly 'One fine day,' That was it. That was the song. It never occurred to me to ask her how she knew; I was just so relieved to know what it was called and to grab hold of the tune that had been rolling around my head.

Some days later, while thinking of something completely different, a memory popped into my head out of the blue. I was about five years old and had woken up with a bad dream and rather than deal with me upstairs, my mum had brought me downstairs where she and my sister were watching a film. As I sat bleary eyed on my mum's knee, her favourite song 'One fine day' was playing on the television.

I had never remembered that memory until that moment and it just made me think, *'Well, what else is in there? What other things have I got buried in there waiting to get out? Was now the time to find out?'* I had always been interested in how or why we turn out the way we do, is it nature or nurture, what effect does the way we live affect the way we are? So, that is how it started and here is where it has ended. You hear people when describing events in their life as saying that they have been on a journey and depending upon your perception, you either think, well ok or what a load of old rubbish. I have to say that writing became something that I needed to do rather than anything I wanted to do.

I wrote my first book then about my first fifteen years of life and although I never had it published, it did two things; firstly, it helped me grieve and secondly, it made me realise that I did indeed love to write, and in some instances, need to.

I really believe that I love to write because of where I came from, my culture and my roots and maybe something else.

My first real memory was of me standing looking over the edge of our bathroom sink, I was about four at the time. To call the room I was in a bathroom was a bit too grand really. It was all pink and black, not the porcelain of course, only the paintwork, which I suppose was all the rage in those days. It consisted of a bath, a sink and a wooden chair in the corner under the window; I do not think we even had any curtains, but I may be wrong a four-year-old's memory is a bit suspect but it was opaque glass, so that is okay whatever the recall. There was no toilet in there, that of course was outside. I was a bit scared of the bathroom which was weird, the fear of inanimate objects, very strange. It was probably because the only time I ever went in the bathroom was on a Sunday night when I had my weekly bath, usually with my older brother. The rest of the time I got washed in the sink in the kitchen, if I could not avoid it, so bathing and the associated bathroom became a trigger for something to be avoided, if at all possible, it was also extremely cold in there when you were naked. Also on Sunday nights, which had become a bit of a ritual, after my dreaded bath, I had my fringe cut by my dad. He had to do it because my mum could not cope with the disaster of two car flicks and widow's peak. I had to sit very still on a chair in still in front of the fire in the living room, sitting still in itself was a trial, while my dad attempted, but never quite achieved, a straight line across my forehead.

The reason I was in the bathroom that time was because I had been extremely ill all over my teddy bear, and my bed I presume, but I do not remember that bit, just trying to get the teddy clean. I was stood at the sink with tears streaming down my checks, I was so little I could not see over the top of the bowl but I was determined I was going to get it clean as it was the only teddy I had. We did manage to get it clean, me and my mum, but it would not dry out, as there was no central heating in those days, just a coal fire in the living room and one in the front room on a Sunday. Aunty Lizzie across the road did not even have a fire; she had a range that provided the heat and cooking facilities. When I used to go over there, I remember how she used to heat the iron up on top of the range with the clothes airing on a maiden at the side. Anyway, I finished up getting a new teddy from my sister's friend because my old teddy was hung out on the washing line for that long that my mum decided it was never going to dry.

My second memory revolves around the watching of 'Watch with Mother' on BBC1. I would be about four at the time and after lunch, I would sit and actually watch it with my mum. Bill and Ben, the Flowerpot Men, Andy Pandy and my all-time favourite on a Friday, The Wooden Tops and 'Spot', the dog. Mum would sit on the settee and I would curl up on her knee with the heat of the fire on my left cheek and the warmth of her bosom on my right and I would fall asleep to her singing:

Jesus bids us shine,
With a pure, clear light,
Like a little candle,
Burning in the night,
In this world of darkness,
So let us shine,
You in your small corner,
And I in mine

I lived with my mum and dad and older brother in a terrace house on Drury Lane in Oldham. We did use to live at number sixty-one behind the bookies. Apparently, when we lived there, we did not even have our own outside toilet; we had to share one with another family, but I do not remember that; I only remember living across the road at number ninety. It was after the war and it was a case of needs must but before I was born, the family moved to the bigger house across the road. It was a rented house, which meant that when my dad separated the front bedroom (it was my brother-in-law who did the work actually, but my dad told me it was him) to gain an extra room, he could not build the wall up to the ceiling. It was against tenant rules or something, but it did have a positive side, it enabled me and my brother to talk to each other over the top even though we were legitimately still in our own bedrooms; you cannot get in trouble for that.

My dad (brother-in-law) also built a partition in the front room downstairs, so that we had a lobby after the vestibule. The first door on the left off the lobby took you into what was now the front room proper. We only used the front room on a Sunday because that was the 'best room'. I always found it a bit dark and dingy to be honest, probably because it only had a fire lit on a Sunday. When you entered, there was the fireplace in the middle of the far wall with two brown leather type upholstered chairs at either side, one for Mum, one for Dad. I always used to have recurring nightmares about those chairs, do not know why but they seemed to scare me, strange, being scared of front room furniture. They were second-hand, of course, as we never had new furniture, it was after the war, after all, somehow pieces just used to appear but I never knew where they came from. On the opposite wall to the fireplace, was the settee and to the left was a radiogram which played 78s, 45s and 33s.

Mum's pride and joy was in the right-hand corner of the room, a cocktail bar. It was a monstrosity in shining rosewood consisting of two cupboards in the bottom, bowed doors of course, and a dropdown section at the top with mirrors and lights and everything; we used to turn the big light off and use it as a substitute for a table lamp. In the dropdown part of the bar were different types of miniatures, glass cocktail sticks from Eastbourne pier where they made them in front of your eyes and paper umbrellas that Mum had brought home from Blackpool. It is a good job she did not try and drink the miniatures because most of the contents had been substituted with cold tea by my brother. Behind the front room were the living room, kitchen and backyard and upstairs were the dreaded bathroom and three bedrooms.

My two older sisters had got married, left home and had families of their own, the only other relatives that lived near was my nana and aunty and uncle.

My nana lived with my aunty and uncle. I do not remember much about her except for two things; she was bedridden when I knew her and she used to open and close her bedroom curtains with an old rusty rapier she kept in the corner. I have no idea where she got it from. She also used to bang on the floorboards with it to get my aunty or uncle to get her things. The second thing I remember was her box of jewellery; I think it must have been her that started my love of jewellery, trinkets and all things glittery, quite a magpie. When I used to visit her, I would sit and play with her collection while my mum talked to her and Nana would always say, "You can have that when I die."

I do not think at that point I knew what dying meant. I had not ever met anyone who then died, I did not even know my other grandparents. I did realise it was something bad when my mum used to say back, "Oh, don't be so silly," in a way that I somehow understood that my nana was not being silly.

I did get the box of jewellery when she died but only half full, my aunty had the other half.

This aunty was my dad's eldest sister; she married my uncle and they had a son who went to live in Cape Town. I never met him but I saw the photographs and the two stag heads with real fur that had pride of place on the wall near the door. I always had a grotesque fascination with them.

Every Friday night after my nana had died, me and my mum used to go to my aunty and uncle's. My mum would make them a hot meal, something like Tatta Ash with a nice big pastry crust. My aunty could not cook, well actually, she used to use a range at her old house but this house was a new council house with electricity which they had been moved into. In Oldham after the war, the emphasis was on trying to meet the need of the shortage of homes, this included the massive clearance of older unfit houses like my aunty and uncle lived in. The first post-war estate that built was Fitton

Hill in 1955 but my aunty and uncle did not live there; they lived in one of the one thousand, six hundred and forty-five new homes built in Chadderton and Failsworth. My aunty had never used electricity for cooking before and just did not know what to do and the new house did not have a range, so they just made do. It never entered my head to wonder what they ate the rest of the time; I just took it for granted that we went on a Friday night.

I had trouble with my aunty and uncle; well, my uncle really. Not that he ever did anything to me, in fact, he hardly took any notice of me, which was normal, nobody did. It was just that he was a bit of an embarrassment to me, not that I would ever had said anything like that, very rude.

Whenever you went round to their house, my uncle would answer the door, never my aunty. You could hear him long before he arrived to turn the latch. They had oilcloth in the vestibule, their vestibule was not like ours with two doors it was just a space between the living room and the stairs. The reason you could hear him before he got there was because he wore great big hobnail boots, even in the house. He never took them off. Well, he must have had to go to bed.

He was a bit accident prone, my uncle, he had a job in a cotton mill and one day on the way to work across Whitegate Lane, he got hit by a car and broke his right leg. He was off work for quite a while, but I do not remember seeing him at that time. However, after a while, his leg healed and he went to have his pot off at the hospital. All was well and they said that he could return to work. The day after he went back to work and while he was there, he got one of his feet stuck in a bucket, fell down the stairs and broke his left leg.

It did cause some amusement in our house, but not as much though as his big toe. Because he broke his leg, he had to take his boots off; when he broke his right leg, it did not seem to be a problem but his left leg was a different matter. When the offending hobnail boots were removed what was revealed was even more astounding, he had a big toe nail that must have measured more than three inches. No wonder, he had such big boots, they must have been five times too big.

The question on everyone's lips was "Why didn't he cut it?"

No one knew.

Mum had told my aunty to do it, "I can't," she wailed.

"Oh, don't be so bloody stupid," Mum replied exasperated taking the scissors from her, "let me do it, y'daft bugger." It would not budge.

In the end, they had to get the nurse to do it, she used a pair of pliers and a chisel to get rid of it.

The problem with me was that every time I saw him from then on, the old Dan the Bakers man tune came into my head.

Dan, Dan the baker's man,
Washed his face in a frying pan,
Combed his hair with a donkey's tail,
And scratched his belly with his big toenail.

I would have been in serious trouble had my mum known, not only was it very disrespectful to think about my uncle in that way, but to even think the word 'belly' was very rude, it was stomach. I did argue that stomach button in place of belly button just did not sound right, I was told it was a 'navel'.

My uncle's leg healed and he could go back to work, I suppose he got a new pair of boots, but I do not know. The only problem was that he had become very wary of traffic and his route to and from work meant crossing the infamous Whitegate Lane. He took to crossing it with his hand outstretched holding and waving a white handkerchief in a form of surrender. I was horrified. Whitegate Lane was on my way to senior school, what would I do if my crossing the road coincided with his? I would just pretend I did not know him.

Although as a child, I made fun of my uncle and was mortified by his use of the white handkerchief, I think on reflection that they both should have been applauded, not ridiculed, they had tenacity and they 'got on with it' through massive and probably very scary and stressful change. I believe that this tenacity is also a part of my behaviour engendered by the culture around me and from my mother.

I never had a broken bone like my uncle and do not remember being ill very often but besides that my mother had the northern woman's view on sickness, just get on with it.

"Mum, my legs fell off."

"Oh, don't worry, it will be alright when you get to school."

I believe living after the war had a massive impact on me, not that I survived the war, I was not even born, but that there was a resilience built into you even though you probably did not realise it at the time.

"What have you got in your hand?"

I had just entered the house carrying a drawing pad under my arm and my mum was looking at me like I was in deep trouble.

"Desert Rat give me six-pence to get it," I replied sheepishly.

"Vivienne Booth, you are in serious trouble when your dad gets home. You do not beg," Mum said in the way that I knew she would forget about it before my dad got back.

It was the summer holidays and I was a bit bored. I had already asked my mum for a six-pence for a drawing pad and she had said no, so I had gone out in to the street in a sulk. I was sat on the pavement just outside my house. I did not sit on the step as I normally did because my mum had just polished it with red cardinal and it was gleaming in the sun, besides I might get piles. This was something I had trouble with, my mum did not tell me what these piles were, I realised they were not a load of dirty washing or a stack of bricks, but what were they? I puzzled a long time about that one. Anyway, I did not know what on earth they were except that they were bad and you had to look out for them. Mum only used red cardinal on the front step but not on the back step because no one but us would see the backyard, so she covered the back step with donkey stone and drew a line round the first two big flagstones in the back yard. Donkey stone was a kind of yellow colour, you wet it and then you had to use your hands to get the colour even on the flags. It got the name because it was a stone and a man with a donkey brought it round the streets, obviously.

No one was around, my brother was out on the window cleaning round with my dad and none of my friends were playing out; I was fed up. As I was flicking a stone up and down the hopscotch court, I had chalked up a couple of days earlier, Desert Rat walked up from the bottom of our row of terraced houses. He was called Desert Rat because that is what he was in the war. Deserts Rats got their name in the sands of North Africa in World War Two. Adolph Hitler had prepared for war by socially engineering his followers into the 'perfect' fighting machines. Identifying with his authority, they obeyed him rather than thought about what they were doing. They had been conditioned to die for their nation's glory even if this entailed sacrificing their own life and the lives of their mates. They were aggressive, strong, without empathy and at the outbreak of World War Two, they crushed all who dared stand in their way.

But in northern Africa, the Germans confronted a very different breed of soldier; they found soldiers without respect for authority or for domineering powers. Most of these soldiers were volunteers without dreams of glory but who instead believed that some things were worth fighting for. They were empathetic soldiers who were infuriated if their leaders brushed aside their suffering or dared express an attitude that any man was expendable or inferior. They were mainly from Australia and at Tobruk, they gave Hitler his first taste of defeat. Great Britain withdrew most of its forces from Africa and sent them to defend Greece leaving the Australians with the task of defending the portal city of Tobruk. Desert Rat must have been one of the English soldiers left behind. Whenever I saw him, he always looked sort of smart and wore a blazer most of the time; I do not think he had any medals or anything on it. There was something strange about him, you would think him being a hero and all, that people would respect him but they did not seem to, they always avoided him and whispered about him. He never spoke to me and I kept out of his way, he was a bit funny.

"What's wrong wi you?" He asked.

I was a bit surprised, in fact I looked up at him with my mouth open so wide, it looked like I was catching flies, I was a bit scared of him really. "Nuffin," I mumbled.

"What y'shrickin for then?"

"I am not crying, I want a drawing pad and me mum says I can't have one," I replied mortified that he thought I was crying.

"How much are they?" He enquired.

"Six-pence."

"A tanner?" He said more to himself than me, he then fished in his pocket, took out a six-pence and threw it to me on the floor and then walked off without a word. Well, I was astounded. I knew I should shout after him and explain that I was not allowed to take money from strangers, but then he was not a stranger, he was Desert Rat. Yes, but that was it, he was 'strange' and besides he was someone I was not supposed to talk to, never mind take money off, but I really wanted a drawing pad. By the time I had thought all this through in my head, he was gone, so it was too late I told myself, mind you, with a bit of effort I could have run after him, but I did not. Instead, I went to the paper shop and bought the drawing pad. I was not that daft; my mum might take six-pence off me to give back to Desert Rat, but she would not give him a drawing pad.

I never could get this taking money off people rule right in my head. It was like Whitsun. We were quite poor really, as were most people around us, it being after the war and a window cleaner does not earn a massive wage, so we did not get new clothes very often, but at Whitsun we did. We would get a full outfit, not normally from a shop that I can remember but actually made for us and on Whit Sunday morning, we kids would put on our new clothes with pride. For my part, there was always a bit of apprehension mixed in with the pride because I would always be traumatised as well on Whit Sunday as that would be the signal to cross over from long socks back to short socks, I hated it. To be perfectly honest, I hated the change back from short socks to longs socks with equal venom. There was one infamous year that my mum completely threw me and decided that because my legs were so thin that I should wear white knitted stockings to plump them up, you know the usual 'your legs will look fatter in them'. Well, there was a slight problem here. I did not have a suspender belt, so I spent Whit Sunday and many subsequent Sundays with my hand permanently up my skirt pulling my knickers up. My mum had attached the stockings to my knicker elastic via four enormous safety pins.

Once we were dressed, we would go round to our neighbours to show off our new clothes. Now these neighbours were pre-selected by some undefined selection criteria that I could never quite fathom, they were not all of our neighbours, just some. We would go in and give them a spin, show them our new clothes and they would give us money. I do not know why they did this but I did not complain because I was allowed to spend it on myself in whatever way I wanted to. After the visit to the neighbours, we would all walk round with the Emmanuel Church Whitsun procession, even my mum and dad and my sisters and their families came, we would all end up for a service outside St Andrews Church near Broadway. Then, we would all walk back to our church, but if we saw anyone, we knew from the inner money paying circle on the way back, we would get some more pennies from them. Why was this not begging?

It was also like the lead up to bonfire night, in those days you did not go 'penny for the guying', you went 'cob a coaling'. For a couple of nights before bonfire night, you and your friends got your guy and went knocking on people's doors, when they opened it, you sang to them:

We come a cob a coaling for bonfire night,
Your coal and your money we hope you enjoy,
Frol-a-dee, frol-a-daa, frol-a-diddle-I-doo-day,
Done in yon cellar, there's an old umbrella,
And done in yon corner, there's an old pepper pot,
Pepper pot, pepper pot, morning till night,
If you give us nowt,
We'll steal now't and wish you goodnight.
If you haven't got a penny, an'apenny will do,
If you an't got an'apenny, then God bless you.

A bit like carol singing really, then they either gave you some money or they did not and what you got from them, you grouped together and bought fireworks with. But that was not begging either.

Contemplation of these events made me realise that it was about community, supporting each other in small ways and the positivity of 'getting on with it' which seemed to be a massive theme.

I do believe this ingrained culture helped me deal with what happened when my mum and dad died and losing the one thing I had left, Red my dog.

The problem was I could not take Red to where I was going to live, and no one but me wanted him. Fred, my cat was to go and live with my brother's girlfriend's mum, she said she'd have her (Fred is a girl), I did not have a problem with that, her mum lived in Diggle in the countryside and it would be good for a cat, but what about Red?

A friend of my dad, Jeff, came to the rescue and turned up trumps. He had heard that the landlord at the Britannia Pub at the top of Coalshaw Green Road wanted a guard dog. The Britannia was opposite where my aunty used to live before she moved to her council house and it was where my eldest sister used to have a sing song on a Friday night, playing the spoons and using an upturned stool as a drum. Not as good as Mrs Tweedale at the Albion Pub across the road from us I should think, but a good night out, just the same. That would be good then, Red would like it there.

Jeff had brought the news about the pub and the guard dog when he came to pay his respects for my dad; he even brought his own collie dog with him. My sister was not very impressed, she was even less impressed when passing a cup of tea to Jeff in my mum's best China, he let the dog drink out of his saucer.

I went to the pub with Jeff on the Saturday lunch time, I was so upset, Red was all I had left and I was giving him away. Not only that, I was giving him away literally, no one took him for me, no one thought that it would be seriously difficult for me; I do not think they even thought about it, he was not wanted and so he had to go, I just had to get on with it. I was not going to let anyone see I was upset though. I was being brave. We took Red into the backyard of the pub with the landlord in tow.

"I'll have to tie him in't garage, love, or else he'll git away cos gate's th'open."

I just nodded and looked at Red as the landlord chained him to a wall in the garage.

"Look, he'll be well fed," he said as he threw him a big piece of steak.

I nodded again. I could not speak; I had a lump the size of an orange in my throat and my eyes were stinging like mad but I was not going to cry in front of them. Red looked so confused and he just did not know why I was leaving him with this strange man in a place he did not know.

Jeff stayed for a pint in the Brit and I walked home down the long backs, so no one could see me crying, I sobbed my heart out. When I got home, my eldest sister was there and she gave me a hug. I needed that hug. A couple of hours later, Jeff arrived back at our house with Red. I was amazed. Jeff had gone to the outside toilet at the Brit before setting off home and had found the landlord kicking Red; Red had been howling like mad because he did not know where he was. Jeff threatened to hit the landlord, untied the dog and brought him back. Not a bad bloke, after all. We found Red a home on Aunty Amy's grandson's farm and even though I was losing him, I was a lot happier about it although I still missed him, he was the last remnant of everything I knew.

I think it was this event over anything else that moulded the person I became and that along with the ingrained tenacity, positivity and resilience made me who I am today.

Did it make me want to write?

Yes, partly, but it is also the need I have to explain and more importantly to be heard. It is not just from my mum and my surroundings that has engendered my love of writing but it is massively what else I have inherited from those early years and that is my dad's absolute love of telling stories.

Cromer November 2020

Yay! I have just received a letter to say that I have gotten a publishing contract for my first book.

IT IS NOT ALWAYS EASY, BUT THAT IS LIFE. BE STRONG. KNOW THAT THERE ARE BETTER DAYS AHEAD.

Ingram Content Group UK Ltd.
Milton Keynes UK
UKHW010723070423
419773UK00013B/1025